New Baptists
New Agenda

New Baptists
New Agenda

Nigel Goring Wright

paternoster
press

This book is dedicated to

the members of the Baptist Union of Great Britain
who elected me their president 2002–2003

and

the members of Altrincham Baptist Church, Cheshire,
who welcomed me as their senior pastor 1995–2000

First published in 2002 by Paternoster Press

08 07 06 05 04 03 02   7 6 5 4 3 2 1

Paternoster Press is an imprint of Paternoster Publishing,
PO Box 300, Carlisle, Cumbria, CA3 0QS, UK
And PO Box 1047, Waynesboro, GA 30830-2047, USA
www.paternoster-publishing.com

The right of Nigel Goring Wright to be
identified as the Author of this Work has been
asserted by him in accordance with
Copyright, Designs and Patents Act 1988

British Library Cataloguing in Publication Data

A catalogue record for this book is available from
the British Library

ISBN 1-84227-157-1

Cover design by NineFourZero
Typeset by Textype, Cambridge
Printed in Great Britain by
Cox and Wyman, Reading

Contents

Preface

The appearance of this book coincides with my period of service as president of the Baptist Union of Great Britain for the year 2002–3. My tentative hope however is that it might become a resource for thinking about the identity and direction of Baptist churches throughout the first decade of this century. If it does it will, from my perspective, have been well worth the effort. In preparing it for publication I have felt a bit like a bricklayer. Some of the bricks that have been brought together here have been used before and are now being recycled. To make them fit I have had to chip off some dried cement that was used previously, and smooth the odd rough corner. Other bricks have been baked specially, although even one or two of these contain clay that has served other purposes in the past.

Roughly half the book has a textual prehistory, sometimes a complicated one. Chapters 3, 4, 5, 7, 8 and 9 (the core of the book) were delivered as The Burleigh Lectures in Adelaide, South Australia, in August 2001. I am grateful to the principal of Burleigh College, Dr Stephen Spence, for his and his staff's hospitality and friendship on that occasion. Even then, chapter 7 had been delivered in Oxford in a previous form to the Joppa Group, concerned with interfaith relations, in April 1999. Chapter 8, having been delivered first of all to the postgraduate research seminar at Spurgeon's College, then appeared under the title 'Inclusive Representation: Towards a Doctrine of Christian Ministry' in the *Baptist Quarterly* in its

October 2001 edition. Chapter 9 had an outing at the Christian Ethics Study Commission of the Baptist World Alliance at its meetings in July 2001 at Charlottetown, Prince Edward Island, Canada. Chapter 6 was also delivered as the C. R. Batten Lecture in Bloomsbury to the London Baptist Preachers' Association in November 2001. All these chapters have been reworked, sometimes extensively, for this present volume. I am grateful for all the comments and discussions that have enabled me to express my ideas more clearly as a result of previous use of these materials. I owe my thanks to Professor John Briggs, editor of the Baptist Quarterly, Dr Spence and the LBPA for kind permission to re-use this material here.

I am also grateful to Dr Robin Parry of Paternoster Publishing for his interest in this project and his expediting of its publication. As the reader will have noticed the book is dedicated to the members of the Baptist Union of Great Britain and in particular to our friends in Altrincham Baptist Church in Cheshire.

Dr Nigel G. Wright
Spurgeon's College, London
Advent 2001

1

Legends of the Fall

This book is basically a book for Baptists by a Baptist. In saying
this I reckon that I immediately risk cutting down its sales
potential. However as there are at least 80 million Baptists in
the world, many of them English speaking, perhaps it does
stand a chance of selling a few copies. In fact it is the second
such book that I have written and I still receive requests for
copies of the first one, now long out of print. In 1991 I
published *Challenge to Change: A Radical Agenda for Baptists*[1] as a
contribution to a growing debate among Baptists in England
and Wales about the health, shape and future of their
particular way of being church. It was widely read, at home
and abroad, and made a modest impact upon a process of
rethinking and reforming that came to something of a climax
at the beginning of 2002, the year in which I assumed for a brief
period the role of president of the Baptist Union of Great
Britain. It seemed appropriate not to update the book but to
produce another one that might give Baptists a steer as they
embark upon a new stage of their lives. Hence the title *New
Baptists, New Agenda*.

My expectations are modest. Indeed the word 'modest' is
one that recurs with a degree of frequency in this book. As I
shall explain at certain points, I do not expect imminently a
reversal of the fortunes either of Baptist Christians in
particular or of Christianity in general in the nations of the

---

[1] Eastbourne, UK: Kingsway, 1991.

British peoples. I can share the hopes and aspirations of those who look for 'revival' but frankly doubt it is going to happen, or at least not soon, and certainly not in the form that some would like it. These are less dramatic and more humble days. But once we have come to terms with this there is much to do in order to ensure the health of our churches and our discipleship and the transmission of the faith to the next generations. Productive, faithful and creative Christian living is possible for us, and the church of Jesus Christ, with all its failings and sometimes precisely because of them, is still a fascinating project, which, despite all voices to the contrary, will endure from generation to generation and is set to surprise the world with its resilience. And, yes, there are many small but encouraging signs of spiritual life that those who have eyes to see can truly discern.

Tracking the 'True Church'

For much of their existence the various competing tribes of the Christian faith have expended quantities of energy excommunicating each other. Where the 'true church' is to be found, and where it is not, has been an issue about which every branch of Christianity might be expected to have a view. Even in these ecumenical days, how true 'ecclesiality' (that in which the essence of the church consists) is to be defined continues as the subtext of much interchurch dialogue, albeit couched in much more refined and polite language than may once have been the case. Baptists too have been part of this debate. For them the true church is to be found where Christ is present, and this in turn can be detected by the presence of certain external signs: true doctrine so that we might know in whom to believe; the experience and confession of heartfelt faith through which Christ is appropriated as Lord; the gathering of believers in the name of the One who is worthy of faith and who makes himself present; baptism and the Lord's Supper as indispensable signs and seals of his salvation; openness to the

Christ who is present not just in one local congregation but in many. As a Baptist all of this makes sense to me and seems credible, as might be expected. These characteristics are of the essence and other matters (ordained ministers, bishops, buildings, special days, church structures, hymns, songs, liturgy) however valuable for the mission and well-being of the church are not ultimately its essence. Give me a minimalist version of what really makes for church any time. In that way we may avoid the error of trying to 'unchurch' people who in God's eyes truly are church.

Believing that our branch of church just happens to be the 'true church' whereas the rest are 'unchurch' or at best 'subchurch' is a luxury that nobody can afford any more. For a start, it just is not believable. Patient attention to the witness of the Christian Scriptures makes it more and more clear that the 'essence' of church was being incarnated and contextualized in a variety of ways even before the ink on the New Testament parchments was dry. Equally, patient cross-cultural observation of the diverse ways of being church to be found in virtually all parts of the world dispels the illusion that *our* group is the *true* group. The dynamic life of the Spirit of Christ keeps on cropping up even where our human imaginations insist that it has no right to! Insistence that we have the true church is exposed by the hermeneutics of suspicion to be just another attempt to bolster our self-centred, self-interested, self-serving occupation of power and privilege. It is astonishing, though not surprising, how theologians who would divide the world into the elect and the reprobate never locate themselves amongst the reprobate. And apocalyptic, visionary movements who speculate about the descent of the New Jerusalem usually have it coming down in the place where they just happen to be living at the time – Ashton-under-Lyne being the most intriguing candidate that I have come across (and yet, why not?)! Human beings seem not to be able to stop putting themselves at the heart of where 'proper Christianity' is to be found.

It is time to grow beyond the parochial competitiveness of

the past and it is possible to do so without falling into the opposite immaturity of thinking that anything goes and no one thing, or belief, or practice, is better than any other. It ought to be possible to argue that some things are good but that others are even better. To say one thing is best is not to dismiss or reject any alternative as being worthless. It is simply to be discriminating and to give hope of progress.

The True Church is Yet to Come

Here is the main thesis for this opening chapter: *None of us can claim to be the true church, because the true church has yet to come.* The true church is that company of all peoples and tribes and tongues that will stand before God at the last. It is an eschatological community that has yet to emerge, yet to be gathered, yet to be seen. The church that currently exists is but an anticipation, but a genuine one, of that universal gathering of all those who through all ages will have been gathered by the Spirit through Christ to the Father in order that God may be all in all to them. Until that day everything falls short and is less than 'true', even as it is genuine. It may well be the case that the church that exists has 'tasted the powers of the age to come', but this is a foretaste and a down payment of a future that will surpass all our imaginings.

This book begins therefore by adopting a futurist perspective on the church and will attempt to sustain that focus at various points along the way. The future defines us. What we are moving to, travelling towards, is what constitutes our true being. We are a people of promise and hope. This does not mean that there are not many things to be learnt from other parts of the Body of Christ in the present: quite the contrary. It does mean that, having learnt things about ourselves by means of comparison and contrast with others, what we have learnt needs then to be interpreted in the light of the future towards which we are all moving. No part of the church of Jesus Christ has 'got it': we are all pilgrims on a journey, fellow travellers towards a destiny that is as yet only partially realized. The treasure is always in clay pots. There is no room for romanticism about other parts of this pilgrim church; the grass is not greener on the other side of the hill, nor even on the hill beyond that. Neither does this future perspective mean that there are not many things to be learnt from the past. The past is very important, not least because a movement that does not have a past probably does not have a future either. Those who do not learn from the mistakes of the past are doomed to repeat them. But it does mean that we should not let the past ensnare us. Memories play strange tricks.

In the story of the Hebrews, God led his people out of captivity in Egypt into the Promised Land, as he had promised. But the going got tough and the people complained (repeatedly) in the hearing of the Lord: 'If only we had meat to eat! We remember the fish we used to eat in Egypt for nothing, the cucumbers, the melons, the leeks, the onions, and the garlic; but now our strength is dried up, and there is nothing at all but this manna to look at.'[2] Here is an extraordinary example of the power of nostalgia. Indeed, the food fantasies always seem to me to be a pretty convincing culinary reason for not going back to Egypt! But they thought otherwise and the apparent absence of kebab houses in the wilderness was a blow to them. Through rose-tinted spectacles they viewed their past lives in Egypt and it was transformed from a place of bondage into one of bounty. By contrast manna, God's specific provision for the present moment, was despicable. In the name of an ill-remembered past they despised God's gifts in the present moment.

Legends of the Fall

Romantic memories of the past, or legends of the fall as this chapter designates them, can turn out to be a distinct

---

[2] Numbers 11:4–6.

hindrance to inheriting the future. To be sure, the Bible and Christian theology operate with a very important legend of the Fall. Christian interpretations of Genesis 3 speak of a fall from original righteousness and communion with God into a state of multiple alienations – from God, ourselves, other people and from creation itself. Death enters the human race as a result of disobedience on the part of the first human or humans and its repetition by subsequent generations. The idea of the Fall and original sin functions as a criterion by which to judge the state of humanity – we are fallen away from the intention and the potential contained in our creation. This state of fallenness, or lostness, is a powerful analysis of the human condition. But the use of this motif becomes unhelpful when it is assumed that therefore salvation and restoration consist in being taken back to the state from which we originally fell. Salvation must be seen as far more than this – it is the way in which God by entering, in the person of his Son, into our fallen condition brings us back on track to inherit the future that had always been purposed and planned. Salvation is not just the restoration of the *status quo ante* but the fulfilment in Christ through grace of the potential that had never been entirely forfeited but that had been suppressed by the disobedience and disbelief of humankind. The Fall should be seen not only as an historical occurrence but as the fact that we have all sinned and fallen short of the glory of God, missing God's design and purpose for our lives. Yet through God's saving work that glory will be fulfilled in Christ in the future consummation towards which we are being drawn by the Spirit of God.

The future therefore has priority and is the means by which we make sense of our present journeyings. For this reason, among others, the resurrection of Christ has such significance for Christians. The resurrection was the manifestation of the power of the age to come. It was the glory and freedom of the future age appearing in the midst of time, thereby declaring that Jesus Christ is God's ultimate servant in whom we may securely place our trust. Ultimate reality has dawned in Jesus and he is the one through whom we too may enter into the power of the age to come. He is God's agent for the world's salvation and we live in the life that he makes available to us. To celebrate the resurrection is indeed to refer back to a past event in history but even more so to look forward to a future of which that event is a foretaste. This discussion is intended to shape the way we think about all aspects of Christian truth, to orientate us towards the future and to do so not least in the ways we think about the church. When we are backward looking concerning the church we end up arguing. When we look toward the future we pull together to work for the coming of the true church.

I have always been intrigued by a throwaway remark once made by Jesus. He was talking about wine and wineskins and making the point that you cannot put new wine in old wineskins because they will burst. New wine requires new wineskins, and in the same way the new spiritual energy of the Kingdom of God, of which he is the agent, must seek for new patterns and structures to contain it. The old religious and legal forms of Judaism were not adequate for the new spiritual life associated with his coming. For this reason Jesus was not well received by the Judaism of his day. There followed a remark that does not seem to follow logically: 'And no one after drinking old wine desires new wine, but says, "The old is good."'[3] This saying is surely ironic. Jesus is not saying this to approve of it but as an ironic commentary on his own experience, and indeed as a generalization about the perpetual ways in which human beings respond to new things. The old is better; the new is inferior. The way we used to do things is better than the way we are now being asked to do things.

When it comes to church life legends of the fall abound. The old preachers were always the better preachers. The old hymns were always better than these new ones. The old ministers were the real ministers! The loss of the old ways is presented as something to be mourned. The present days are of inferior

---

[3] Luke 5:39.

quality to former days. However, reading the works of those who lived in what you and I might think of as the glory days yields the surprising discovery that as far as they were concerned even those days were days of decline compared to yet previous ages. And so it goes on. Repeatedly the past is called to witness against the inadequacies of the present. As people get older and have more to look back upon the motif that there is a 'glory that has departed from the world' grows stronger and recurs more frequently. In times of reform and change the weapon of nostalgia is trundled out to resist and despise it.

As this book is for and about Baptists it is as well to ground the matter in our present experience. The steady changes that have taken place among Baptists in the last decade – changes of mood, style, practice and structure – have left the Baptist denomination substantially altered as it goes into the new millennium. Certain groups or types of Baptists now feel more at home within this denomination than they did and have achieved a modest dominance. Others, who were previously dominant, now feel themselves to be marginalized and at times estranged. The temptation to yearn for a vanished past and to despise the present is at hand.

For all I know of course the past may have been, in specific respects, better than the present. It would be a nonsense to suggest that all change is good change. Some change is definitely for the worse. It is not change but deterioration. The problem comes when you attempt to find a standard by which to judge things. We are thrust back upon subjectivism, upon how we remember things to have been, and in this respect there are no absolutes. We all judge things as we see them and as they appear to us. The past will always be viewed from the perspective of what we ourselves have experienced. Speaking personally, my own entry into the Christian faith and into Baptist church life could not have been at a lower ebb (the church I joined was to close down soon after, but I do not think these two things are connected!). There was no glory to depart – the worship was lifeless, the practices ritualized, the theology (of the church members rather than the pastor) non-existent, the buildings dilapidated, the sense of mission absent. This personal biography leads me to conclude that Baptist church life has been getting better ever since. But the personal biography of others might be very different. They are entitled to their perspective, but it is not one that persuades me since it has never been my own.

If the point were pressed and we were asked to agree on an analysis of the past we would be breaking down into argumentative groups who divided on matters of interpretation without any objective way of mediating between them. This is a fruitless path and will lead nowhere. The crucial question however is not what we have been or how we match up to it now but what we will be in God's future as the true church of Jesus Christ and how we can press on to that goal. The future perspective relativizes the past and the present by placing them both within a sense of God's upward and future call. It democratizes the church because it places us all on the same level – none of us has been to the future yet, however extensively we may have explored the past. It humbles us because we can no longer attach ourselves to past heroes and think that in doing so we are entitled to some reflected glory. They know as little, or as much, about the ultimate future as we do. A future perspective should bring us together in common endeavour for what has yet to be.

Growing into God's Future

A contemporary illustration in the realm of social and political struggle might help us here. While the various political parties in Northern Ireland recapitulate and debate the past they are doomed to go nowhere. The struggle to bring healing to a conflicted society depends for its success on the ability to forget, or at least release, what lies behind and imagine a better future. Everybody has a vested interest in a peaceful and prosperous future and the challenge is to transcend past differences for the sake of a future call. In a very different but parallel way it is this future orientation that Baptists, and indeed all Christians, would do well to adopt.

What does this future vision come down to? In essence it is to do with the church being that community in whom God makes his dwelling. As the persons of the Trinity, Father, Son and Spirit, indwell each other in communion and mutual self-giving, so the church, which is baptized in the name and into the life of the Triune God by the Spirit, is called to live in God and be indwelt by God in full and perfect communion. The people of God throughout the world already experience this in anticipation but not in perfection. It is supremely in this future sense, as an act of faith and anticipation, that we can declare our belief that the church is one, holy, catholic and apostolic. *One*, because it is impossible to dwell in God and not share in the unity of God and the communion that flows from this. *Holy*, because to dwell in God is to participate in the holiness and reflect it in utter availability for God that comes as a gift rather than an achievement. *Catholic*, because those whom God indwells will be drawn from all reaches and corners of God's creation and will express its diversity and difference. *Apostolic*, because the God in whom the church lives and whose purposes the church will continue to serve is the one who is revealed in and as Jesus Christ and that church will accord to perfection with the testimony safeguarded to the apostles. In so far as the church is currently one, holy, catholic and apostolic these are mere anticipations of the true church that is yet to be revealed. In so far as these qualities are only partially realized in the present age they indicate how far the church has yet to travel and the modesty with which it should view itself.

Revisiting Baptist Identity

Let us root this in current Baptist reality before embarking in the chapters to come on more specific topics. I have come to see that *identity* is a crucial issue for all people. Christians have often, not unreasonably, been taken up with matters of truth and reality – how can I find a foundation of truth upon which to build? How can I be sure that I know what I know? Perhaps we have neglected the equal importance of matters of identity. I was struck when someone once said to me: 'The older I get the less sure I am of what I know – and the more sure I become of who I am.' Which is the better of these two possibilities? Who I am is a prior question to how I should live. It is not unrelated to matters of truth since identity rooted in illusion is a snare rather than an assistance. But how I live, ethics, is bound to spring out of a sense of place, purpose and distinctive calling. If I know who I am I shall live according to my self-knowledge. It is not in vain therefore that Baptist Christians over the last decade have debated the issue of 'Baptist identity' and the related issue of 'evangelical identity'. In various ways this book takes up, once more, the issue of identity. My proposal is that Baptist Christians know themselves to be among the people of Jesus Christ and of the God he makes known. They have placed their faith in Christ and have as a consequence undergone a conversion experience that makes him the centre of their lives and communities. This is expressed in baptism as a responsible and believing act. They are travelling patiently and sometimes hesitantly towards a future that he will make known and which they perceive in visionary form as a new heaven and a new earth. As they do so they are guided by the Scriptures (which they regard as the written means of access to the mind of Christ), by a story drawn from their own history (which they regard as a true insight into the Scriptures and so into the mind of Christ) about what the church should be as a believing community, how it relates to society and to state, and by its way of discerning, along with other believers, how the mind of Christ may be interpreted for today.

The rest of this book puts some flesh on these bare bones, and positions Baptists in the British context in relation to some of the currents, movements and questions of the present day as we journey towards becoming, along with all who are in

Christ, the true church of God. Not everybody will agree with
the way I seek to position Baptists and I expect some vigorous
debate from left and right. But in a sense that is the point of the
book. It is a bid to define Baptist identity at the beginning of
the twenty-first century, to position this movement
theologically and ecclesially for the next stage of the journey,
and yet to do so, I hope, in the spirit of friendship as well as of
conviction. I make no grandiose claims for this movement to
which I belong but assert that it has a significant role to play in
the mission of God. It needs to take itself seriously in a spirit of
modest awareness of all that it is not and all that it could be. As
they say, the best is yet to be.

2

Assuming the Position

Baptists are evangelicals – of that there should be no doubt. For this reason Baptist identity and evangelical identity are closely related issues. I begin this chapter with such a bold statement since the close family relationship of Baptists and evangelicalism is sometimes questioned. Past debates and rhetoric have often made the assumption that British (or more accurately English) Baptists can be divided up into 'Liberals' and 'Evangelicals' (the initial capitals are significant) and that these are the two wings of the denomination that (if seen positively) enable us to fly. The complexities in such a contrast are legion and I resist the characterization strenuously. Rightly understood you cannot be a Baptist without being *some kind* of evangelical but, as we shall see, there are indeed different kinds.

The complexities begin with the observation that many who would call themselves Liberals are, in my experience, anything but. There is nothing quite so intolerantly illiberal as a dogmatic Liberal. Those who might define themselves as Liberals can also be astonishingly conservative in their distaste for modern methods and approaches, so ending up on the reactionary rather than the progressive wing of the movement. If anything, the 'legends of the fall' melancholy is particularly to be found among them. On the other hand, as a self-confessed evangelical (note here the lack of an initial capital), I find myself characterized as a liberal from time to time because I do not subscribe to certain points of view that someone somewhere has decided define what 'real' evangelicals look like.[1] I do not mind this – this is more their problem than mine. Some people regard themselves (or others) as liberals because they cannot accept, for instance, the unity of Isaiah or the Mosaic authorship of the Pentateuch. The word 'liberal' is not for me a dirty word if what it designates is generosity and openness of thought and attitude. But there is a difference between being 'liberal' and being a 'Liberal' (the capital letter and the noun form make the point). The latter suggests a set of dogmatic beliefs on a par with any other set of convictions, and it is here that 'Liberals' can be as dogmatically intolerant as any others. On the other hand the adjective 'liberal' is always a relative term. We are all always more liberal than some and more conservative than others. Speaking personally, on some points I insist on being conservative and on others rather more liberal. Other people may quite legitimately place me, if they choose, on a scale of liberal veering towards conservative. The true contrast among Baptists however is not between being Liberal and Evangelical (since these are not binary oppositions) but between being more or less liberal or conservative within the framework of a broad but commonly embraced evangelical faith.

In this chapter therefore I argue several points:

- Baptists are inherently evangelical
- The word 'evangelical' needs to be understood on a broader front than is often the case: Baptist churches are a coalition of emphases within evangelical boundaries
- In Baptist church life a distinctive and healthy form of evangelicalism is increasingly coming to expression, which holds together what some others would thrust apart
- This developing position is where we should *intentionally* position ourselves by developing a new theological and doctrinal seriousness

---

[1] For example, Oliver Barclay, *Evangelicalism in Britain 1935 – 1995: A Personal Sketch* (Leicester, UK: IVP, 1997), 117.

Baptists are Inherently Evangelical

I could argue this from history, constitution and theology. Baptists are a development of Reformation Christianity and grew in the first instance out of the Puritan movements of the sixteenth and seventeenth centuries. It was their desire to be true to the biblical witness not only in their view of salvation but also in their fidelity to the pattern of the church made known in the New Testament that was their inspiration. The heart of the Puritan approach concerned a reading of recovery, a return to Scripture beyond the corruptions of tradition, to reappropriate God's authentic Word and will for the church. The distinctive convictions that constitute Baptist identity involved the restoration, in contradistinction to the majority churches of their day, of biblical motifs that were held to be binding precisely because the authority of Scripture was higher than the authority of tradition.

We may therefore think of Baptist theological identity in the form of several concentric circles. The innermost circle contains the distinctively Baptist combination of convictions: the doctrines of the sole headship of Christ over the church; the church as a fellowship of believers; believers' baptism; the competence of the local congregation; freedom of conscience; and the separation of the church from the state so that it might be self-governing. All these are directly rooted in the New Testament as the normative and binding witness to God's will for the church. Yet this circle is bounded by another since historically Baptists represent a movement in the tradition of the Reformation with its emphases upon Scripture alone, Christ alone, grace alone and faith alone. And these emphases are only themselves to be understood within the still wider circle of catholic Christianity as defined by the normative ecumenical creeds of the first five centuries of Christian history. Movement beyond these boundaries calls into question whether persons or churches may legitimately call themselves respectively Baptist, evangelical or Christian.

This is one reason why I am reluctant to admit that Liberals (back to the initial capital!) represent a legitimate party within the Baptist spectrum. Historically, Liberal Protestantism has called into question or attempted to reinterpret the fundamental doctrinal formulations of Christian faith, such as the Trinity or the deity of Christ, in such a way as to make it difficult for those who hold fast to the doctrinal tradition to recognize in it the apostolic faith of the church. By contrast, all the historic confessions of the Baptists have made clear, and have often been written *in order* to make clear, that they belong to the mainstream of Christian faith and confession. Baptists belong to the strand within the Christian tradition that arises with the evangelical churches of the Reformation and then diversifies into a variety of positions mainly concerned with the nature of the church.

Precisely this is reflected in the constitutions of many Baptists churches and certainly in its 'model trusts', which indicate that Baptist churches 'hold to the authority of the Holy Scriptures and that interpretation of them usually called Evangelical'. This wording has recently been called into question on the grounds that no definition of what constitutes 'Evangelical' has been agreed and probably never could be. What is at issue here is partly a misunderstanding of what this phrase means. It does not imply, as some have taken it to do, that there is an agreed evangelical *doctrine of Scripture* to which Baptists must adhere. Rather, it is a reference to the *content of Scripture* as interpreted in the evangelical tradition. Negatively, therefore, it is to be distinguished from other traditions of interpretation, such as Roman Catholic, Orthodox or Unitarian. Positively it is to be located within the tradition of the Reformation with its characteristic emphases upon human fallenness, justification by grace through faith, the once-for-all sacrifice of Christ and the proclamation of the Gospel.

In this sense the word evangelical is intended as a meeting ground for those who might disagree on a variety of issues but share a 'mutually recognized theological tradition and a common ethos and polity'.[2] Historically it entered the vocabulary of Baptist churches in the revision of the constitution of the Baptist Union that took place in 1832 and which aimed at extending mutual 'love and union among Baptist ministers and churches who agree in the sentiments usually denominated evangelical'.[3] In this usage the term emerged as a broadly conceived replacement for the more detailed and restrictive Calvinistic confessions that had been used to that point. On the basis of this more inclusive alteration, the New Connexion of General Baptists, which was Arminian in theology, was immediately enabled to grow closer to the Baptist Union and then to merge with it in 1892. It is important to notice that the function of the term 'evangelical' has been to permit those who might otherwise disagree to find common ground in a general tradition of faith and commitment for the purposes of mission. At the same time it is an important boundary word and the omission of the phrase 'sentiments usually denominated evangelical' from the 1873 revision of the constitution appears to have been one of the aggravating factors in the later Down Grade Controversy that badly damaged the Union in 1887–8.[4] Then as now the term implied both the characteristic *content* of belief and the outward-looking *practice* of evangelism. The term still has this value in allowing a latitude of belief within identifiable boundaries of conviction and faith.

Theologically speaking, however, we need to give more attention to the word. Some years ago I wrote an article for *The Guardian* in which I argued that the Labour Party (which was at that time distinctly in the doldrums) might do well to look for new recruits within the growing body of evangelicals in the country. The correspondence that followed included a letter from an Anglican priest who obviously regarded evangelicals

---

[2] Ernest A. Payne, *The Baptist Union: A Short History* (London: Carey-Kingsgate Press, 1958), 254.

[3] Payne, *The Baptist Union*, 61.

[4] Payne, *The Baptist Union*, 130–1.

as a recent and alien import from America. He demonstrated both that he was ignorant of the tradition of his own church and that he shared a common stereotype of evangelicals as right-wing Fundamentalists. This is very far from the truth but illustrative of a point: the recent, post-World War II revival of conservative evangelicalism is mistaken for the broader evangelical tradition, which has its various roots in the theologies of the Reformation, Puritanism and continental Pietism. I am not denying that conservative evangelicalism is part of that tradition (it is – and it would deny being 'Fundamentalist'), simply that it is not the whole of it. If it is true that evangelicalism is in some significant respects a product of the Enlightenment, it is also true that its linear forebears are the main churches of the Reformed tradition. Far from being simply a party within the Protestant churches, as indeed they often regard themselves, evangelicals are in fact in direct continuity with the main concerns of the Reformation itself and can lay claim to being its faithful descendants. We grasp this point more clearly when we remember that the preferred self-designation for the Protestant Reformers is 'evangelicals' and that the German word *evangelisch* is how the German Protestant churches still describe themselves. In a similar way, in the nineteenth century all British free churches designated themselves as evangelical and many were united in the twentieth century into the Federal Council of Evangelical Free Churches,[5] a precursor of the more recent Free Churches' Council.

Evangelicals in Coalition

Baptists are inherently evangelical and have historically embraced the word as a way of describing themselves. The

---

[5] A 'Declaratory Statement of Common Faith and Practice' for this project was accepted by the Baptist Union Assembly in 1918 and sets out the doctrines that were then associated with being an evangelical body: Payne, *The Baptist Union*, 275–8.

overwhelming majority of Baptist churches today acknowledge this and affirm it. But we have seen enough to argue that this evangelical identity needs to be broadly conceived. From its origins in the Reformation the evangelical tradition has in fact been a broad coalition of those with Lutheran, Reformed and Anabaptist sympathies. The passage of time has served only to broaden this out further, not least with the growth of renewal and Pentecostal movements and the spread of the church across the world. Evangelical Christians have had to come to terms with a variety of perspectives among those of similar mind even while vigorously advocating their own! Increasingly therefore evangelicals have seen themselves as existing as a series of tribes held together by family resemblance and by strong relational ties and loyalties. Amongst Baptists, the growing together of General and Particular Baptists with their Arminian and Calvinist emphases constituted a basically evangelical denomination with a tolerance for different approaches. There will always be an argument about what the acceptable boundaries of this tradition are and what exactly belongs to its irreducible norms – it is evident that you cannot believe just anything and still claim to be part of it. But within these boundaries there is room for a broad coalition of conservative, radical and liberal evangelicals representing differing approaches and emphases within a commonly owned tradition.

The ways in which these approaches might differ have often been understood in relation to the use of the Bible. Conservative evangelicals have been suspicious of many of the results of critical biblical scholarship, have generally wished to maintain traditional views of authorship and composition, and have above all argued for the historicity and facticity of the biblical record. Liberal evangelicals have been more accepting of critical scholarship, more willing to accept that not all the Bible needs to be given the same historical status but that it is replete with symbolism and metaphor, and more aware of the diversity of emphasis within the biblical canon itself. Radical evangelicals have been impatient with endless debates about the Bible when the Bible itself calls out for action to set the oppressed free – biblical people are those who engage in the struggle for justice as well as those who call people to personal conversion.

As with many aspects of Christian thinking, the tension between the varying emphases outlined can be seen as part of the process of dialogue and debate that is itself of the essence of Christian reflection. Even in the biblical canon there is a variety of emphases. The Bible is an unfolding narrative of events and their interpretation does not proceed uniformly but dialectically, in the form of continuing affirmation and questioning through which growing insight and a witness to God's activity emerges. Debate amongst evangelicals, as amongst Christians in general, is essential in discerning the truth. As with the canon, there are boundaries to be reckoned with, but room within them for 'contest'.

A Distinctive Form of Evangelical?

I would hesitate before saying that Baptists represent a unique kind of evangelical since, when it comes down to it, there are many others who are travelling on not dissimilar roads. However, it does seem to me that something distinctive, although not unique, may indeed be happening. Not a few evangelicals have wanted in recent years to describe themselves as 'post-evangelical', having come to question aspects of the theology and religious culture in which they have received their spiritual nurture. The term appears to me to be problematic in that to be 'post' suggests that identity is being negatively defined – 'this is what we were but we are no longer quite so sure what we are.'[6] As a word it tells us where people may be coming from but not where they are going to –

---

[6] See on this my article,'Re-imagining evangelicalism' in Graham Cray et al., *The Post-Evangelical Debate* (London: Triangle, 1997), 96–112.

this could be a dead end. For progress to be made something more positive needs outlining and this, for Baptists, must be in the form of a reimagined evangelical theology.[7]

A broad judgement on changes amongst Baptists over the last twenty years would be that the denomination has become more evangelical ('moved to the right' is another way of expressing this perception, but not one I welcome). An equally accurate perception would be that British evangelicals in general, including Baptists, have 'moved to the left' both theologically and politically. The predominant form of evangelical faith expressed by Baptists is a long way from the separatist, non-ecumenical, individualist variety familiar among Baptists some years ago and still to be found in the independent evangelical sector. Baptists therefore tend to express a centrist form of evangelical life and witness, which, in general terms, is progressive, ecumenically open (but not particularly enthusiastic about formal ecumenism), holistic in its approach to mission and often profoundly engaged in social action and regeneration projects alongside evangelism. Divisive politics amongst Baptists has vanished almost to the point of invisibility. This brand of evangelicalism could be described by the use of various adjectives, but the neat categories of 'conservative', 'liberal' and 'radical' with which I began this chapter are probably no longer adequate to describe what is, on the whole, a healthy ferment. 'Open', 'unitive', 'ecumenical', 'catholic', 'progressive', 'mainstream' and 'centrist' are all possible adjectives to describe the kind of evangelical faith being formed. The consequence of this ferment is that individuals are increasingly difficult to label or stereotype.

---

[7] As one helpful contribution to this see Stanley J. Grenz, *Renewing the Center: Evangelical Theology in a Post-Theological Era* (Grand Rapids, Michigan: Baker Academic, 2000).

Using the Bible

One major aspect of this new ferment relates to biblical interpretation. Conservative evangelicalism has had a tendency to argue theological issues by giving careful attention to the biblical texts on any given issue on the assumption that all texts carry equal authority as the Word of God and that interpretative distinctions made on the basis of 'who said what' are invalid. Decisions about biblical truth are made on the basis of weight of textual evidence and in the weighing process Paul carries as much authority as Jesus because he speaks under the inspiration of the same Spirit. As a recent example, the Evangelical Alliance report on hell discusses the matter of 'eternal torment' following just such a methodology.[8] This could be said to be consistent with the basis of faith of the Evangelical Alliance, which maintains 'The divine inspiration of the Holy Scripture and its consequent entire trustworthiness and supreme authority in all matters of faith and conduct'.[9] The Bible is the final authority and so the balance of what it says is decisive. In an apparently minor but actually hugely significant variation on this, many evangelicals (including many who, like myself, belong to the Evangelical Alliance and read its Basis of Faith in a somewhat different way) affirm another methodology for interpreting Scripture. In this Christ is seen as the Word of God to whom the Scriptures give normative access in their written testimony. Hearing the Word of God requires listening to the Word of God as spoken in Christ and as the Hebrew Scriptures have prepared us to hear it and the Greek Scriptures to recollect it. The Bible is to be interpreted *christologically*, with Christ as the key for interpreting and reading the whole. Reading and heeding

---

[8] *The Nature of Hell: A Report by the Evangelical Alliance Commission on Unity and Truth Among Evangelicals (ACUTE)* (Carlisle, UK: Paternoster, 2000), 77–95. It also devotes a chapter to the theology of hell.

[9] Article 2, Evangelical Alliance Basis of Faith.

every part is important, but the Bible is not a flat book with every part of equal significance: Christ is the centre and makes sense of the whole. This leads to a different approach from the balancing of texts in that it inclines the discussion of disputed issues in a more theological direction. The Bible is read through Christ who is the clearest revelation of the Father and from this core a theology of the Triune God emerges in the light of which the individual texts of Scripture may be understood in true perspective. It is still true that the texts must be wrestled with but a more theological approach to the interpretation of Scripture will sometimes mean that they are treated more metaphorically than literally.

This way of reading the Bible has its parallels and precursors not least in the theology of Karl Barth and in the hermeneutics of the Anabaptists.[10] It is also reflected (knowingly or otherwise) in the Declaration of Principle of the Baptist Union of Great Britain, which asserts 'That our Lord and Saviour Jesus Christ, God manifest in the flesh, is the sole and absolute authority in all matters pertaining to faith and practice, as revealed in the Holy Scriptures'.[11] One commentary on this asserts:

> Now, this phrase of the Declaration makes us different from some other evangelicals . . . We have always honoured the Bible as the Spirit-inspired gift of God to his people, the reliable place where we can expect to hear the living Word of God. But we read it and we interpret it, with the help of the Holy Spirit, as witness to the one who is the Word of God in the fullest sense.[12]

I suggest that learning to interpret the Bible increasingly in this second way has shaped the kind of evangelical faith and

---

[10] See Stuart Murray, *Biblical Interpretation in the Anabaptist Tradition* (Kitchener, Ontario: Pandora Press, 2000).

[11] Article 1.

[12] Richard L. Kidd (ed.), *Something to Declare: A Study of the Declaration of Principle* (Oxford: Whitley, 1996), 29.

witness currently being expressed amongst Baptists. It has helped provide a centre ground among conservative, liberal and radical evangelicals and to break down older hostilities. It has at the same time caused some from the 'right' to move to pastures new, because they prefer another approach to biblical authority, and some from the left to drift away because they are more indifferent to biblical authority anyway. It has also helped to render obsolete a long-running debate about the relative priority of evangelism and social engagement. Christ the Word gives us no option other than to hold these together. Baptist evangelicals do hold these together and are demonstrating themselves to be extensively engaged in social regeneration while not losing their commitment to evangelism.

A New Theological Seriousness

As this chapter is entitled 'Assuming the Position' I can come clean about my conviction that this 'centrist' or 'catholic' evangelical position is a healthy place to be and that it should be intentionally affirmed as part of Baptist identity at the beginning of the twenty-first century. It provides a way forward for our development in a way that is not true of 'post-evangelicalism'. It allows us to be faithful to what we have received whilst facing up to the challenges of the present and future. It requires us to be thoroughly Christ-centred in theology and discipleship. Moreover it means potentially that rather than Baptist Christians being theologically defined by movements and trends originated by others, they might increasingly develop as a distinctive and creative theological variation within the broader evangelical rainbow. However, there is another interpretation of recent history that merits careful attention. Could it be that the greater sense of theological cohesiveness among Baptists derives not from a renewal of theological perspective and conviction so much as from a simple indifference to doctrine?

There are significant signs that Christians in the West

generally have shifted towards a more experiential and less doctrinal expression of their faith. This would be in keeping with the general 'postmodern' cultural climate, which is supposedly sceptical about 'metanarratives', and with the impact of those enthusiastic movements identified as Pentecostalism and the charismatic movement. In addition, Bible reading among Christians, including among those who supposedly have a high theoretical view of the text, is in decline year on year. The levels of biblical literacy among Christian people are likely at the present time to be lower than they have been since the invention of the printing press. If there is a new tolerance among Baptists around issues of doctrine might this not be that we have simply slipped into anti-intellectualism? If so it must augur ill for the future. Movements can only survive if they have ways of recounting and transmitting their faith. Theology and doctrine are the means by which faithful Christian ways of believing are interpreted for the modern world in order that it may gain access to faith. Without them we are left with sentimentalism or undifferentiated mysticism. Although all theology will reflect the context in which it is undertaken and will take up its particular concerns, there is a normative and abiding core to Christian belief, and to Baptist convictions, which needs to be recovered, re-expressed, celebrated and transmitted. Only so can we avoid being taken captive by the transient trends of our various contexts. The way it is done is by passing on the 'pattern of sound words'[13] that has been entrusted to us.

It is a paradox that in an age when Christianity in the West is in decline, Christian theology should be undergoing something of a renaissance. Far from it being the case that serious theology has been sidelined, forgotten or over-whelmed by pluralism and secularism, there is a body of believing theological teachers and professors at work today that surpasses in quality many preceding generations. Many would describe themselves as evangelical and many others as

---

[13] 2 Timothy 1:13.

orthodox Christian believers. When all has been said by the passing and sceptical theologies of the later twentieth century, theology is able to return to classical Christianity and find in it a vitality and wisdom that surpasses the wisdom of the age. This is demonstrated by the breadth and variety of recently published works in the area of Christian doctrine. There are first-class resources available here for those who have opportunity to study and research and for those 'regular' Christians who wish to understand their faith more fully.

Stanley Grenz and Roger Olson describe the theological enterprise taking place along a spectrum stretching from folk theology through lay theology to ministerial, professional and then to academic theology.[14] If folk theology is a collage of ideas and images quite unrelated to Christian beliefs, and academic theology is often preoccupied with philosophical matters with no direct relation to the life of the church, the three central aspects of the enterprise are of huge importance. Lay theology arises when ordinary Christians dig deeply into the resources of their faith and join heart and mind in living out the Christian confession. They may lack the sophisticated tools of biblical languages and an extensive library but they are engaged in serious theological reflection. Ministerial theology is the reflective faith engaged in by those who have received training and recognition for forms of ministry, ordained or otherwise, within the church. Professional theologians are those whose vocation it is to provide the training and education on which others may draw. Of these varying kinds of theological activity it is perhaps lay theology that needs to receive a new prominence and impetus in order to establish the church as an intelligent and insightful presence within the community.

It is vital for Baptists to tap these resources and to enter into a new age of theological seriousness. This, of course, is never an alternative to Christian experience. It goes alongside it to

---

[14] Stanley J. Grenz and Roger E. Olson, *Who Needs Theology? An Invitation to the Study of God* (Leicester, UK: IVP, 1996), 27–35.

give depth and stability to it, to enrich it with resources of the mind and of the tradition. It will nourish Christian experience in times of emotional barrenness and confusion. In addition it will enable Christians to make their witness in the world with intelligence and thoughtfulness and so to lend persuasiveness and moral force to their mission. It will give weight and authority to the Christian voice.

My own experience is that in the wake of the movements of renewal over the last twenty years many believers have been left hungry for understanding. It is as if when people first come to faith they build a mental box to provide a framework for their new experience of Christ. This serves them well enough for a number of years. But life is complex enough to challenge any box and after a while the box no longer seems to square with life as it is lived. At this point what happens is crucial. Either they work on their box again and improve on it, so that it can cope with the questions they have learnt to ask, or they lay aside the faith as no longer adequate for their needs. This is tragic, given the intellectual depth and resilience the Christian faith has displayed throughout history. The resources available are more than enough. What is needed is a culture of learning that enables people to love God with all their minds as well as all their hearts. If Baptists could be known for both their evangelical zeal and their theological competence they would justly gain the respect both of the believing and unbelieving worlds.

3

The Courage to be Modest

Big tasks await the church of Jesus Christ. In the last century, despite the decline of the church in the West with which all of us are familiar, the growth in the universal church has been nothing short of exponential. Much of that growth has been on the wing of the church that Baptists in part represent: the radical, believer-baptizing wing. I mention simply the emergence and growth of Pentecostalism to make my point. The church is not going away. The influence of Jesus Christ upon persons, cultures and nations is greater than it has ever been. The largest of all the tasks that confront us concerns the shape and practice of mission in this new day. How can the redeeming power of Jesus Christ be extended beneficially into this world? We would be quite wrong to assume that we know either what mission is or how it should be done. We need to think again, and to think well.

What Mission is

The ready evangelical assumption is of course that we do know what mission is: it is evangelism, telling people about Christ so that they might put their trust in him and what he has done and so pass from spiritual death to spiritual life. This would not, of course, be untrue. Evangelism in these terms is indeed at the heart of what we should do. But such evangelism is not everything that belongs to mission, nor is it everything we have assumed it to be.

For instance, some more catholic sections of the church speak not of evangelism but of 'evangelization'.[1] The difference amounts to more than a preference for Latin-sounding nouns. Evangelization is the proclamation of the truth of Christ not just to persons but to cultures. In the redeeming work of Jesus Christ creation is brought to its true goal. The work of salvation is at the same time therefore a revelation and an uncovering of the true nature of creation itself. In the message of salvation is also the fulfilment of creation. For this reason every part of the human endeavour needs to be evangelized, whether this be the civic or political realms, the worlds of music, literature and the arts, of work, or of industry and economics. If indeed it is the case that all things are to be reconciled to God through the Cross of Christ (an astonishing claim, but there it is in Colossians 1:20), then the proclamation of Christ is as broad as the world itself. It is global, holistic, universal, all-embracing. Christians are to be people who have universal sympathies and universal vision, shaped and informed by the Christ they confess and the God he makes known. After all, if Christ is indeed the one through whom all things have been made, the *logos* who was with God in the beginning of all God's works, and is their origin, what he has done for us in the course of a human life must make its impact upon everything. For the agent of creation to become part of that creation in order that it may experience new creation must have universal implications and impact. As the good news of Christ is proclaimed so it works its way upon culture and brings about change that makes for good.

Rejecting False Dualisms

This allows us no space for what are sometimes called 'dualisms', where two realms are pitted against each other. So, a view of salvation that sees it as the saving of the soul from

---

[1] David Bosch, *Transforming Mission: Paradigm Shifts in Theology of Mission* (Maryknoll, New York: Orbis, 1992), 409–11.

the body is a false dualism. We are to be saved in our entirety: body, soul and spirit as the doctrine of the resurrection makes plain. The idea that the whole purpose of God for us is that we 'get to heaven' neglects the biblical vision of the renewal of all things in the new heaven and the new earth. The assumption that the only things that really matter are those that take place in the 'sacred' realm of the church while 'secular' reality is worldly and beyond the pale misses the fact that 'God so loved the world' that he gave his only Son to participate in it and redeem it.[2]

Yes, evangelism/evangelization is far more than personal conversion – but it is certainly not less than that. One trend in the West, faced with unresponsiveness and apathy towards the message of the church and the feelings of irrelevance that this evokes, is to redefine salvation. So salvation is seen primarily in corporate and political terms; as participation in those movements that make for liberation or emancipation from oppression. So, the thinking goes, we may not see conversions, but we don't really need to. As long as we can feel ourselves to be contributing to the onward march of the cause of freedom and justice we can believe we are doing God's work.

There are things to applaud here, but there is also huge reductionism. Salvation embraces the reconciliation of people to God, the coming home of the lost and wandering to discover new life and favour in the Father's house. And the bottom line is this: if people are not being converted to Christ to become lifelong disciples of their Lord, who will there be to throw themselves into the fray of social action and the struggle for justice? It cannot be taken for granted that there will be Christians in the next generations – they have to be made, to be won to personal commitment and allegiance.

Back we come again to the matter of holistic mission. To be in mission is to be sent by God to do God's work, indeed, to be swept up by the Spirit of God into that which God has been

---

[2] John 3:16.

doing since the beginning of time and does supremely in Christ: seeking and restoring that which was lost – all of it, persons, cultures and creation itself. To be converted is to be drawn by that Spirit into the community of God's people, which is sharing with God in this task, and to be incorporated as part of it. It is to work with God for the fulfilment of God's purpose: living out and speaking out the good news of Christ. This embracing and generous vision of our calling is what the church needs as it turns face forward to face the future.

Unpacking 'Modesty'

But let me come at this point to what ought to be the most intriguing word in the title of this chapter. It is the word 'modest'. Nothing in the language I have so far employed disposes us to be modest. The concepts and the language I have offered are universal and totalizing. The claim of Christ comes not just to some people but to all people; not to one *ethnos* but to all *ethnoi*. It comes not just to people but to cultures and communities, not just to the animate creation but to the inanimate. It embraces all of history and all of time. All things (a characteristic Pauline term) were made through him and for him. All things are to be reconciled to God through him. This is total, triumphant and all-encompassing in scope and expectation. Where is there the need, or even the room, for modesty?

As an orthodox Christian I believe both that the Christian faith must be confessed anew in each generation and that it is *the Christian faith* and not some pale substitute ideology that needs to be so confessed. Continuity and renewal are both important. The word 'modest' needs to be understood therefore as a reference not to the doctrinal content of the faith so much as to the style and manner with which we hold and advocate that doctrine in the contemporary world. We are more likely to gain a proper hearing for our faith (in the Western world at least) if we adopt a position of modest advocacy rather than of strident dogmatism. Modest and sincere conviction will achieve more than aggressive confrontation. Moreover, there is the 'courage to be modest' in this sense.

A discernible tendency in the modern evangelical church, whatever may be true elsewhere, is to meet the discouraging nature of the times by talking in a loud voice and sometimes 'acting big'. Several times over my years in ministry great excitement has been generated by predictions that revival is almost upon us. Sermons have been preached, books written (and sold at some profit), conventions have been held by means of which modern Christians, teetering on the brink of profound discouragement, have been bolstered and energized by the expectation that an imminent reversal of fortunes is upon us. Indeed, as a preacher, I know well enough the need to have something to offer people, to mobilize them and motivate them by offering a project, or a teaching, or a practice that will make available to them something to invest in, a means to something better. In the light of this it actually takes a certain kind of moral courage to say that perhaps these things are not going to happen. Perhaps our calling for the time (in our parts of the world at least) is not to triumph but to endure. It takes courage because in a subculture that is used to talking things up it might sound like defeatism to talk things down. Such realism might, to be sure, be taken as a ground for complacency or inaction. Against this I would argue that actually the reverse is more likely to be the case. As the proverb says, 'Hope deferred makes the heart sick.'[3] There is nothing more discouraging than continually being offered predictions that do not in fact come to pass. Better to recognize that although in some ways this is a day of small things it is not therefore to be despised.[4] At such a time there are things that can be achieved, things that are in themselves good and that hold open the promise of something better.

---

[3] Proverbs 13:12.
[4] Zechariah 4:10.

Powers, Principalities and Atmospheres

I confess to having been impressed in this regard during a visit to Cuba in the year 2000 to attend the General Council of the Baptist World Alliance in Havana. I visited churches and was encouraged to see people responding in some numbers at the end of the quite traditional service to the message preached. I heard of other meetings held over the week, often addressed by Westerners, at which the same response invariably took place. I was intrigued to learn from the pastor of the church that in five years Baptist congregations have grown from 15,000 to 45,000 members. Even more interesting was the fact that this growth has been happening since Fidel Castro addressed the Baptist leaders in the early 1990s and said to them, 'You have been persecuted and this was wrong. I give you my word that this will never happen again.' What I learn from this is that where there is lack of growth it is not necessarily because the message is wrong or the preaching lacks eloquence but because the atmosphere by which the church and its preaching are surrounded is resistant to that message. Indeed, although I am far from in agreement with the popular notion of territorial spirits, the element of truth within such a remythologizing framework seems to me to be precisely this: there are powers around us that remain open to or resistant towards the Gospel of Jesus Christ, and these are not under our control. They affect what we do. The church in Cuba had to endure many years of relative numerical stagnation before the atmosphere changed and a new day of opportunity opened up.

In the West it is a change of atmosphere that is needed above all. Whatever comments, critical or constructive, need to be made about the church, the resistance of people and their culture to the Gospel is not entirely to be laid at the church's door. It belongs to that wider 'mystery of lawlessness' of which Scripture speaks.[5] There is a complex Opposition to the

---

[5] 2 Thessalonians 2:7.

purposes of God. For the time being the wider culture appears either deliberately or by default largely to have decided against Christianity. Until that shifts significantly the Western church, not by any means for the first time in its history, is likely to be in endurance mode rather than in resurgence. It is a recurring thesis of the Old Testament scholar Walter Brueggemann that just as Israel experienced what it meant to be displaced by the imperial power of Babylon and was sent into exile, so the Christian church in the West is both displaced and exiled by a hugely powerful ideology that constitutes both the ruling agent and the atmosphere of Western and Western-influenced societies. That ideology, which while concealing itself actually constitutes the metanarrative of our culture, he names as 'technological, military consumerism'. He means by this that:

> (a) consumerism is the conviction that the unit of social meaning is the detached individual whose self and identity consist in consumption; (b) such unbridled consumption requires a disproportion of wealth and advantage, which must be defended by military means (for example, immigration policy); and (c) this defense of advantage is readily and simply justified by a one-dimensional technological mindset that in principle brackets out of consideration all human questions.[6]

This is a hugely powerful metanarrative/ideology/princi-pality that is widely dominant and profoundly inimical to the Gospel. To name it helps us to identify both why that Gospel finds little hospitality in such a host culture and what kinds of pressures that culture exerts upon the church that it seeks to make conform to its own image, often successfully. The church is displaced by this rampant and dominant empire. It is thrust into exile. While it endures, and it will not always do so of course, progress is likely to be seen in the small things rather than the greater.

---

[6] *Theology of the Old Testament: Testimony, Dispute, Advocacy* (Minneapolis, Minnesota: Fortress Press, 1997), 741.

It takes a certain kind of courage to make this statement of modesty and to recognize the reality of our situation. Being in exile is not comfortable. However, the scriptural tradition is a lasting reminder to us that exile can be a place of new discovery, of new faithfulness and of considerable renewal. It was under the conditions of exile that the Jewish tradition came to a new place of usefulness in the purposes of God and in its contribution to history. The Hebrew Scriptures as we currently possess them were decisively shaped in exile as Jewish exegetes and prophets reappropriated their own history in the light of the exilic experience. Although a time of displacement, exile can also be a time of renewal. So I take up the theme of modesty. Rather than offer yet another formula for potential triumph I wish to offer a number of reasons why modesty in style and approach should be our watchword in the contemporary world.

The Ambiguous History of Christianity

The history of Christianity is a matter of well-scrutinized public record. It is open to examination by historians and other scholars of friendly or hostile disposition alike. Christianity has been around for 2,000 years and has had ample time to make mistakes and for the implications of those mistakes to be displayed before the watching world. Emil Brunner once wrote a book entitled *The Misunderstanding of the Church*[7] in which he argued that the church is both a heavenly and an earthly community. As a heavenly community there is within it that divine reality that makes it distinctive, but as an earthly community it carries with it all the regular concerns and patterns that would be true of any human communities and institutions. In terms of where we began in the first chapter, the true church has yet to be seen. In the present we have only anticipations of it. The history of the church reveals it to have

---

[7] English translation: London: Lutterworth Press, 1952.

been the playground of power-seekers and abusers, as with any other human arena. It has made alliances and compromises along the way that are not to its credit. It has displayed hostility and prejudice, has been self-absorbed and self-seeking, nepotistic and corrupt, punitive and at times complicit in violence. It has fallen into line with idolatries and nationalisms. Not infrequently, as with German Baptists under the Third Reich, when the church has been at its most 'spiritual', or focused upon the need to preach personal salvation, it has been inclined to ignore and therefore to encourage gross error in the civil and political realms.[8] It has been the 'unfree Free Church'. While proclaiming itself to be the agent of redemption it has itself been in manifest need of redemption. It is useless to argue that when the church has been like this, this isn't true Christianity. Of course, it isn't; but it is the only Christianity that currently exists. It would be tempting to believe that our particular corner of Christianity has been exempt from this ambiguity, and from time to time there are those who yield to this temptation and revise their history to serve ideological purposes. But historical enquiry rarely permits us this luxury and usually subverts our idealized readings of our own history by demonstrating that even the most radical groups are shot through with their own failures.

History can be held against us in a way that renders us relatively powerless. We may of course be able to contest historical readings of our own past and show that there is another side to some of the claims that are made. Philip Sampson has done this very intelligently in his book *Six Modern Myths Challenging Christian Faith*[9] and tackles systematically the claims frequently made concerning, for instance, the church's attitudes to Galileo, Darwin, the environment, the 'heathen', the human body and to witchcraft. But finally, there

---

[8] See Andrea Strübind, *Die Unfreie Freikirche* (Wuppertal, Germany: Oncken Verlag, 1995).
[9] Leicester, UK: IVP, 2000.

is more than enough in Christian history to subvert naïve claims about the church having the answers to the world's problems. The church, often enough, has been part of the world's problems. Far from it being the case that the church will show the world what it means to be redeemed, it increasingly appears that until the world itself, with which we are bound up in the bond of life, is redeemed, the church will still be awaiting its own redemption. Christian witness today therefore is to be tempered by its own history if it is to command a hearing.

The Persistence of Sin in the Church

In a similar way we are confronted by our present reality. In theory the church is set in the world as a sign and a sacrament of divine redemption. In reality, it appears, the Christian doctrine that is given most ample confirmation by the church's life is that of human sinfulness. Whatever new birth and baptism into Christ achieve they do not eradicate the sin that persists in believers. Each congregation in particular and the whole church in its regional and national configurations demonstrate our evident inability to extricate ourselves finally from the matrix of human fallenness. We are contextualized not just in the sense that we inhabit particular cultures and conditions but also in that we imbibe the specific forms of sin that are endemic to our own cultures. We see this more readily in others than in ourselves but what is true of any of us is probably true of all of us. If technological military consumerism is the metanarrative of Western culture then there are few of us who have not bought into it and live out its mores.

Supremely, the church demonstrates the very fragmentation and division of humankind that in its very essence it is meant to overcome. Christian truths become the cause of new divisions rather than the means of overcoming old ones. The eucharist, meant to be a sacrament of one body, becomes the point at which we exclude and excommunicate. The Christian church of the present, leaving aside that of the past, is as much the embodiment of what is wrong with God's world as it is of how it may be put right. Lacking communities that unambiguously embody the Gospel, authenticity requires us to acknowledge that the church is as much a denial of the Gospel as it is its confirmation. When we offer our witness to the world it is not only Christian history that might count against us, but the church which lies open to people's scrutiny today. Ancillary to this is the personal dimension. When I speak as a Christian or as a Christian minister I am conscious of my own inability to live up to the Gospel of God's gracious love that I proclaim. For I too am one who is shaped and defined by my experience of God's grace but also by my fallen and as yet unhealed humanity. I am not therefore free of the potential to use spiritual realities as a cloak for my own self-preoccupation.

Simple Answers in a Complex World

The offering of a prophetic Christian witness may be jeopardized by the actual reality of the church, but also by the simple fact that Christian 'prophets' appear to be saying different things. If the church has the answer, it appears to have different views on what that answer actually is. Attempts at Christian prophecy range from those inclined to the right, who interpret the needs of the present predominantly in terms of personal morality, and the left-inclined, for whom oppressive structures account for most of the world's ills. The claim that Christ is the answer to the world's problems may be true, but being true does not make it simple. *How* Christ is the answer to issues most of us barely begin to understand appears to be less than straightforward. How the interpretative transition is to be made from a first-century Christ to a twenty-first-century world involves a number of sophisticated thought processes. Most of us do well to doubt our own ability to read both the complexities of present realities and the

biblical text sufficiently authoritatively as to make pronounce-
ments.

'Absolute Truth' in a Postmodern World

Finally here I draw attention to a debate with which most of us
will have some degree of familiarity and which usually passes
under the heading of 'postmodernism' or 'postmodernity'.
That we are all in postmodernity strikes me as a matter of
simple chronological fact. It is the general context within
which we live out our lives and there is no doubt that the
Gospel has to be spoken into this kind of age. This is not to say
that all who live postmodernity subscribe to a philosophy
known as *postmodernism*. Within our postmodern world all
manner of philosophies, some of them distinctly modernist,
continue to survive and thrive, and many of us flit from one
mode of thought to another as the occasion or the topic
requires without feeling obliged to be totally consistent.
Whereas I suspect that a final definition of postmodernism will
elude us, so that there will always be some hesitation about
who or what we are actually describing, the general contours
of postmodernity seem to be clear enough. One of these is a
general suspicion of any 'metanarrative' that claims to give the
total interpretation of everything and thereby succeeds in
excluding from consideration a whole range of other voices or
perspectives that may have something to offer by virtue of
their very dissonance or difference.

From a Christian perspective this may or may not be seen as
threatening. A range of opinions seems to be on offer
extending from the nihilist who denies that anything exists or
has meaning (rendering language a tool for creating merely the
illusion of meaning) to the view that reality may exist and may
indeed have meaning, but that at best we will only ever hint at
it by means of the language we use, and none of us will ever so
be able to capture it that we exclude all others from having a
meaningful voice on it. If the first end of this spectrum is

manifestly excluded by the Christian story, it appears to me that the latter end is both compatible and commensurate with it. I indicate here my preference for that epistemology that Paul Hiebert defines as 'critical realism'[10] and in which he affirms the reality of a world independent of human beings and capable of being known, and yet which human language will only ever imperfectly interpret and reflect. There is objective reality but it is only ever subjectively apprehended.

From a theological perspective we may indeed believe that we indwell the reality of God, of reconciliation to God and redemption through Christ in the power of the Spirit. Christian language will however always remain a partial and therefore constantly improvable reality. The more we understand about the nature of language the more we grasp that it is shaped by specific experiences, contexts and cultures and that no one form of expression is going to be equally valid universally. There will remain a *diastasis*, a distance, between the reality of God and the language we use to witness to God. The realism that is affirmed here is therefore a critical realism in that the limitations of our concepts and words will always be before us. 1 Corinthians 13 seems to be making the same general point. To some extent this discussion reflects an older debate about the nature of the Bible as the Word of God. Karl Barth argued that it is the Word of God, but only in the sense that it remains constantly the place where the event of the Word of God may happen. Human language is both *adequate* to serve the purpose of bearing witness to God, but simply because it is *human* language it is always at the same time *inadequate*. It is God's grace that makes it adequate. It may become the Word of God. Of itself it is witness to the Word of God, but by grace and through the Spirit it may become the Word of God to us, the place of divine speaking and engagement.

By analogy theological language is of itself witness to divine reality and by divine grace may lead us effectively to that

---

[10] *Missiological Implications of Epistemological Shifts* (Harrisburg, Pennsylvania: Trinity Press International, 1999), 68 ff.

reality, despite the fact that it remains inadequate and limited. No theology is absolute. But it may prove to be reliable and capable of bearing witness to the truth as it is in Jesus. In the postmodern age Christians will bear their witness and will do so with conviction and confidence. But they will also be wise if they recognize that however firmly they believe what they believe even they do not have the last word, and that the divine reality will not be exhausted by what they say. Other voices are therefore worth listening to, engaging with and learning from.

Modesty, but not False Modesty

None of the considerations that I have listed here finally disqualifies the Christian church from having a voice in the contemporary world. However weighty the considerations they engender they need not paralyse. What they must do is lead us to a place of modesty. The historical ambiguities of the church, its present failures and our own awareness of our frail humanity mean that the voice with which we speak is tempered. The line that we draw is not between a world that has the problems and a church that has the answers. It is drawn not *between* church and world but *across* church and world since there are many signs of the church's complicity with the world, the flesh and the devil, and there are some signs that the world, although fallen, has not finally fallen out of God's grace. God continues to show grace and to manifest it in the world with which we share solidarity, sometimes in ways which shame what may be found in the church. In their witness, Christians speak as much to themselves as to the world around them and while not being apologetic that witness certainly needs to be realistic.

In relation to the truth claims of the Christian faith, it is far from the case that the church needs to be hesitant about the content of its faith. Christian faith has been tested and winnowed for centuries and although the ways in which that faith is expressed and packaged have been renewed and updated with the passage of time and the growth of knowledge, its essential content endures. However, robust confidence in the truth of this faith and its ability to persuade and convince removes the need for excessive dogmatism in style and attitude. Aggression is often a cloak for insecurity. Recognizing that all our formulations of Christian teaching are simply our best attempt to be intellectually true to it and that the search for more adequate ways of speaking goes on, the church's task is to say what it has to say with conviction, humility and grace. The idea of the witness is helpful here, as at many other points. The witness tells of what she or he has seen and known. But the witness points away from herself or himself to another in whom the fullness of the truth resides. The role of the witness is simple and modest, but powerful and essential because it gives access for others to realities that have so far passed them by, a witness that only those with first hand experience are able to offer.

A Concluding Picture

As a final contribution let me offer a picture in words.

Jesus Christ was sent from God and his presence continues to be powerfully known by those who look to him by means of the Word that speaks of him and the Spirit of God who makes that Word persuasive and believable in the world today. Those who are graciously drawn in this way find themselves being forgiven and reconciled to God in a way that changes and transforms them and gives them new life, direction and hope. They are drawn into communities of fellow believers in which they are established through baptism and the Lord's Supper in their faith and enabled to grow in understanding and active service to God. Such communities are vitally important in embodying the continuing presence of Christ for the world and in mediating that presence to the wider community that surrounds them. Despite their inevitable human frailty they offer glimpses of an experiment that is talking place among human beings by means of which people break free from their bondage to idols of human creation and learn to live primarily for the service of God according to the pattern of life made known in Christ. It is an experiment fraught with difficulty from both within and without: from within because no human being lives without personal frailties and temptations; from without because the kind of life exemplified by Christ is in fundamental contradiction to many widely accepted values. In so far as the experiment is successful and the pull of divine grace enables a truly Christian way of living, these communities and the individuals who comprise them can exercise a far-reaching and transforming influence upon their world.

A commitment to live Christianly is accompanied by the verbal witness of the church as it interprets its faith and experience to the surrounding world. The primary aim of such witness is to lead others to the point of personal conversion, faith and renewal so that they also may become active followers of Jesus Christ and come to share in Christ's continuing mission to the world as living members of the Christian community. Further aims closely associated with this concern the continuing embodiment of Christ's healing presence in the world through the Christian community and its acts of social care and the extension of this into the civil and political realms by means of the search and struggle for just, righteous and fair laws and institutions. Some members of the church are especially identified as being gifted to teach, and receive extensive training in the Christian Scriptures and the Christian tradition to enable them to teach as accurately, as persuasively and as wisely as possible. The church's witness is its best attempt to give an account in the language and thought forms available to the Christ who is at the centre of their faith and to everything that follows on from that belief.

As this witness is not always well received, the church sometimes comes into conflict with those who disbelieve their message. However the commitment of the church is to maintain goodwill towards all people of all kinds. Its members are all too aware of their own frailties and failures but believe that the grace of God is greater even than their own shortcomings. Because they believe that God is the God of all truth Christians are open to discover truth wherever it is to be found and so are grateful for points of contact and agreement with adherents of other religious traditions and worldviews. Even so, their witness is to Jesus Christ as one in whom God has made himself decisively and most clearly known and whose work in death and resurrection has brought benefits for all people.

Christians see themselves as total witnesses. They offer their whole lives in the service of God and hope to commend the Christian way through every part of it. They believe that God's claim is upon the whole of life and therefore work patiently towards a day, however far in the future it may be, when this claim will be fully realized. Until that day they are both realistic and persistent in their expectation that personal life, community, and national and international existence are at their best and most humane when they willingly conform to God's will. Recognizing that how this divine will relates to the complexities of human existence is not easy to discern, they none the less believe that Christ is the decisive clue to understanding God's will. Disavowing coercion, force or manipulation they bear their witness by means of the open statement and wise application of the truth as they have come to understand it. While not expecting any privileged position as of right they claim with all other points of view the freedom to state and argue their case and they hope to be heard. Beyond all this it is their belief that the coming of God's Kingdom and the doing of God's will on earth as in heaven is not dependent on their efforts but comes as an undeserved gift of God to them and all creatures in heaven and earth.

In our particular culture at this particular time nothing about this missionary task is going to become any easier. In the West, these are not, generally speaking, favourable times for our message. We require resilience and a long-term perspective concerning God's plan. Things will change, but not soon. As we have noted, amongst the powers pitted against us is consumerism, and it is immensely powerful both beyond and in the church. It is the dominant force in mass culture, the primary glue that holds our societies together. Take the lust for things and for consuming away and we might wonder what we have in common. Caesar had a point about bread and circuses: you keep the people quiet by giving them bread to feed them and circuses to amuse them. It stops them asking awkward questions. The temptation for the church is to play the game – to become consumerist congregations with an appeal to the masses couched in values they can understand. A primary decision we have to make is whether indeed to play the game and to compete for attention as one player in the market. Or, believing that our message is unlikely to appeal to the masses but rather to those who have seen through the consumerist lie, should we not rather style our message more modestly to address the dissenters, the disillusioned, the spiritually rather than the materially hungry? If so, the church should be seen not so much as a triumphant army taking on the hosts of wickedness, but as clusters of partisans steadily and creatively undermining the system for the glory of God, believing that One greater than all things can be trusted to overcome and to establish his Kingdom of justice and peace.

4

New Baptists, New Opportunities

The claim is commonly made that we are in a postdenominational age, which is to say that if Christians once gave their loyalties to certain sets of denominational doctrines and practices with a degree of intention and exclusiveness, they do so no more. Within certain broad categories, large numbers of committed and admirable believers are exceedingly tolerant about denominational labels, apparently able to worship and work happily in a variety of denominational settings and relatively indifferent to the particular forms of church order they are likely to encounter there. This is not to say that all differences have been obliterated, simply that they have been redistributed. If once the churches were distinguished from each other vertically, so that people belonged to specific denominational identities, they are now more apt to be distinguished horizontally. Across the denominations therefore there are Christians and churches that are generally charismatic in tone, or generally evangelical, or generally traditional. Those from one denomination are more likely to be in sympathy with those who share their charismatic, evangelical or traditional concerns and who happen to be in other denominations than with those in their own who do not.

Most ministers are familiar then with the phenomenon of churches that are substantially peopled by members from outside their own denomination. Indeed in the great majority of Baptist churches in the UK, I would claim, you are hard put (more than anywhere else in Europe I have observed) to find more than a handful who could or would describe themselves as 'cradle' or 'pedigree' Baptists. I include myself in this. It is this new freedom, or it could be an indifference, regarding specifically denominational values, that can be described as postdenominationalism.

A few observations are in place before setting out some thinking concerning the renewal of specifically Baptist distinctives within our current context.

Responses to Postdenominationalism

The first thing to be said about this new situation is, who could regret it? In essence, the breaking down of denominational barriers must surely be welcomed as a good and enriching thing. There is one Lord, one faith and one baptism and so for any kind of barrier to be broken down in the church of Christ must be counted a good thing. It is slightly paradoxical that often this new degree of interchange is to be found in that end of the church which is least concerned about formal ecumenism. It has been claimed that the charismatic movement is the most ecumenical movement of the twentieth century. It overcomes the sticking points of formal ecumenism (its debates about mutual recognition of baptism, eucharist and ministry) simply by sidestepping them and proceeding directly to a shared communion based upon a common experience of a mutually recognizable Christ. For historic denominational differences to be relativized by a new awareness of the spiritual life we have in common is a good thing. All are one in Christ Jesus.

A second thing, hinted at in the first, would be to observe that denominations are a somewhat ambiguous phenomenon. As they tell their own stories it would be deduced that they originated in a major issue of principle with a host body, or as renewal movements within a moribund church that chose to reject their testimony, or as communities spontaneously gathered around some fresh light and truth that broke forth from God's Word. All these interpretations have integrity and could be multiplied indefinitely to give an account of the huge number of denominations now in existence. On the other hand they cover over other factors that have also been in play. Richard Niebuhr argued persuasively enough that most denominations originated for socioeconomic rather than theological reasons as a protest against the gullible acceptance by the church of middle-class and stultifying values.[1] Personality clashes, power politics and the desire for self-aggrandizement have played, and do play, their part in the proliferation of sectarian groups. Separatism may sometimes be an inevitable option when the church becomes hopelessly compromised, but it is also frequently a symptom of the narrowness of the human mind and spirit. Theological rationalization can usually be supplied to justify prejudice and animosity. Denominations are both necessary, and arguably useful, and to be regretted, a sign of that tendency towards factionalism that was already beginning to threaten the earliest church.[2]

Thirdly, the relativizing of denominations is in keeping with developments in biblical studies. It has become increasingly clear both in Old and New Testament studies that diversity is as much an aspect of the biblical canon as unity.[3] Within the New Testament writings various tendencies in the development of the church can be discerned, whether in catholic, charismatic or mystical directions (witness the Pastoral epistles, the Pauline writings and the epistles of John, respectively), which when more fully developed will lend justification to varying ways of being church. Varied ecclesiologies might therefore be seen as pointing to aspects of the biblical witness, all with their own places and integrity within the total scheme of things. It becomes increasingly

---

[1] *The Social Sources of Denominationalism* (New York: World, 1972).
[2] 1 Corinthians 1:12–15.
[3] e.g. J. D. G. Dunn, *Unity and Diversity in the New Testament* (London: SCM Press, 2nd edition, 1990).

difficult to claim that any one way of being church is the right way.

Fourthly, this leads on to the point that we are in an age when it no longer seems feasible to claim that one theology and practice of the church is right and all others wrong. Instead there are differing ways of being church that are supported by competing theologies, each of which has its own coherence and integrity. We may indeed wish to argue that one theology has the edge over others but we are likely to find that there are aspects to being church that any one model will overlook. As a consequence we need the enrichment of ecclesiologies that inform, challenge and to a degree complement each other. No one of our traditions is the true church. The true church is something we have yet to become and we need each other's assistance for it to become a reality.

Questions to and for Postdenominationalism

Having made these points, which in their own way affirm the new mood of postdenominationalism, let me now raise some questions about our present situation.

Firstly, although we may be in a postdenominational age, it should not be imagined that denominations are about to go out of existence. There are many reasons why this will not happen, not least financial and institutional. Institutions have an ability to endure through time and to adapt themselves, if only for reasons of survival, to new situations. Many of our churches find when it comes to do with survival that denominational structures are necessary and useful in providing both resources and legitimation in today's world. Indeed there are some compelling reasons why such structures should continue to exist and indeed to thrive. If one of the proper concerns of our generation is the way in which religion can become corrupt and abusive then structures that are capable of bringing a degree of regulation have an enhanced role to play in the future. If the age of postdenominationalism is to be a free-for-all in which, without accountability or institutional connectedness, religious entrepreneurs do their own thing, I would suggest we all have cause for anxiety. Abusive religion is too well documented for us to countenance this possibility. New religious movements typically depend upon a charismatic entrepreneuer operating with the least amount of objective and institutional safeguards. To obviate this, either we utilize existing institutional frameworks or we invent new ones. But to invent new ones is to admit precisely that we are not in a postdenominational age. If personally I have tended with age and experience to become more of a denominationalist it is largely because I have seen how energetic and enthusiastic movements, while vital for us, also have a tendency to become eccentric. What is required is more than personal accountability exercised through relationship since even here the potential for self-delusion is considerable. It is some form of institutional accountability in which objectively defined procedures provide a framework less liable to be manipulated.

Secondly, the postdenominational claim must take account of the fact that denominational structures still function with a high degree of vitality in the contemporary world and are able to gather and mobilize large numbers of people for valuable and productive purposes. The overall situation may be different now but that does not mean that there are no further roles to be played or functions to be fulfilled.

Thirdly, new movements that define themselves as postdenominational often come to display characteristics that can clearly be described as denominational. This is true in England among what are called the 'new' or 'Restorationist' groups that originated out of a strong polemic against the denominations. In a more settled phase of their existence they are coming to assume the character of well-defined, culturally similar and corporately closely allied networks. If these are not denominations it is merely because denominations are deemed to be legally incorporated entities, which the new churches have so far avoided being. In internal terms however they display all the characteristics of the shift from sect to denomination to which Richard Niebuhr drew attention. More interestingly, they demonstrate that there are aspects of denominational existence that are deemed to be of continuing value. Churches, for instance, feel the benefit of belonging to a wider movement in which there are shared direction, shared convictions and commonly owned values. They desire leaders who have credibility and charisma and who exercise leadership across the spectrum of churches ('translocally' is a word that has come to describe this) not least by pointing to creative ways forward into the future. They appreciate the capacity to draw upon resources of personnel and expertise from a wider pool of relationships and contacts. They benefit from a clear sense of identity and mission. In so far as these resources are made available through denominations those denominations have a continuing role in the future.

Fourthly, it needs to be affirmed that the issues and questions out of which denominations have emerged have not gone away. Within the charismatic movement it is indeed the case that the quality of a living spiritual experience can bring people together across theological divides and circumvent for a time the sticking points between denominational groups. However, the fundamental questions of theology never go away. They always abide and must be returned to. Beyond the glow of shared fellowship there are still the hard questions of theological discourse that will raise their heads again in due course. Integral to these are questions about the nature of the church itself that lie at the root of so much denominational proliferation. The phrase 'new Baptists' in the title to this chapter is an indication that even as denominational boundaries become more porous a reappropriation of basic denominational values and identities can be taking place. Of course, they will be being 'reimagined' since no one age is completely like another. But *classical* ideas, rather than transient ones, have the ability to reinvent themselves again and again. Baptists represent a classical position.

It appears therefore that if we are in a postdenominational

age this does not mean an age in which denominations have no role to play. It is rather akin to a paradigm shift in which that role is reframed and reconceived according to the general shifts in perception that govern people's overall view of reality. The continuing contribution of denominations within this new paradigm is still to be made. It will be one in which we may gladly accept the relativization of denominational positions and see the new appreciation of diversity as an opportunity for fruitful interaction in which we learn from those of other traditions and wherever possible allow ourselves to be enriched by their insights, incorporating these into our own way of being church. On the basis of this approach I would like in the remainder of this chapter to argue for at least one way in which the identity of the Baptist tradition needs to be modified, and then to outline ways in which this tradition can speak out of its history to the present with both integrity and attractiveness.

Modifications and Assertions

Whatever the ambiguities of the existence of denominations there are two positives that are worth asserting: (1) they have often borne witness to important aspects of theological truth that the wider church was in danger of neglecting or denying; (2) they have provided opportunities for communion between individual congregations that have given meaning to the catholicity of the church. I am writing this book as a 'Baptist Christian'. That term for me is a useful one. It first gained currency in British Baptist circles as it was used by Dr David Russell, a former general secretary of the Baptist Union. He in turn borrowed it from the Russians, among whom it was common to refer to 'Christians–Baptists'. The use of the term indicates that this is one way, among other ways, of being a Christian. The other ways are to be respected. Being Christian has priority, being Baptist is a secondary variation on this theme. This is the relativization of which I have already spoken. Furthermore, among people of this persuasion, and largely under the influence of James William McClendon, Jr,[4] sometimes 'Baptist' has become 'baptist', in recognition of the fact that those who are called Baptist are in fact part of a broader 'baptist' movement in which common values and perspectives are widely shared although diversely expressed. Sometimes this has also been identified as the 'believers' church' tradition and once more seen as a broad spectrum of groups with commitments such as believers' baptism, religious liberty, the separation of church and state and the self-governing congregation held in common.[5] In this chapter I shall from this point prefer the use of 'baptist' in order to place 'Baptist' identity within its broader context. It is my contention here both that this tradition is well placed to contribute in mission to postmodern society and that it itself needs to learn from the wider tradition of the whole church in specific ways. In both these ways, by means of what it can give and what it can learn, as it undergoes renewal so its impact upon the contemporary world can be viewed with a degree of optimism.

Because radical and dissenting groups have often found themselves on the margins of society they have needed to seek solidarity with those who are like-minded in order to endure. For baptists in the sixteenth and seventeenth centuries this meant that the individual congregations springing up sought to build links of association with other such congregations. Associating and associations were therefore part of their life from an early date. Despite this, it is an enduring tendency of such groups that they fragment. In the debates that surrounded the Reformation the opponents of the Reformers, such as John Eck, quite quickly identified a potential weakness in the position of those like Luther, who stressed the importance of individual interpretation of Scripture. Whereas

---

[4] *Systematic Theology: Ethics* (Nashville, Tennessee: Abingdon, 1986), 19–20.

[5] Donald F. Durnbaugh, *The Believers' Church: The History and Character of Radical Protestantism* (London: Macmillan, 1968).

there is a prophetic heroism in the cry, 'My conscience is captive to the Word of God. Here I stand. I can do no other,' it also opens the door to infinite fragmentation of the church according to idiosyncratic biblical interpretation and the sensitivity of individual consciences. Given this tendency, there are few theological safeguards in this tradition to prevent it happening. Because the local is affirmed as having priority over the catholic and the universal, the sense of the place of the local church within the life of the catholic church is easily lost once combined with the innate human tendency to neglect wider concerns (those things that concern the whole) when involved in the parochial (those thing that concern me). It is an enduring and continually repeated flaw in this way of being church that autonomy becomes independency. Each church does what is right in its own eyes. This is sometimes flaunted as the 'Baptist way' and defended against those who want to 'meddle and interfere' in the life of the local church.

If there is any point at which the Baptist/baptist tradition needs to learn from the wider church it is in the recognition that we are part of a movement sweeping forward through time from Christ and his apostles in the power of the Spirit and that we are eccentric and potentially heretic in so far as we neglect the Body of Christ in all its dimensions. Fundamental openness to other churches is an essential quality for being church,[6] even if each local church has within itself the competence to govern itself. This recognition ties in with what we have noted as one of the continuing potential contributions of denominations. They incarnate a way in which the catholicity of the church, our involvement with one another, may be expressed, provided they remain open to the wholeness of the church of Christ.

If it is the case that churches are at their healthiest when they know themselves to be part of a movement, bound together by common values, drawing upon each other for

---

[6] Miroslav Volf, *After Our Likeness: The Church as the Image of the Trinity* (Grand Rapids, Michigan: Eerdmans, 1998), 156.

encouragement and resources, and looking to leaders who are gifted and qualified to fulfil their calling for the good of the whole, then rediscovering this dimension of church life is long overdue. Denominational leaders need to apply themselves to making it a reality. Its rationale is the same as that which baptists use to validate their understanding of the local Christian church. If the church comes into being and is empowered to be church by the presence of the Christ who is in the midst of the twos or threes who come together in his name,[7] then Christ is also present in the wider church whenever it gathers, in celebration or synod, and the local congregation needs to be effectively joined to this wider church. Relationships between the members of the churches are the means by which this happens. Denominational structures, in potential at least, provide a vehicle for such relating and should be seeking in their own renewal of their mission to be bringing this to pass.

At this point it may help to recap on the argument that we have been advancing. First of all we have welcomed postdenominationalism in so far as it points to a new, larger and more humble awareness of our belonging together as the people of God. Secondly, we have argued that within a postdenominational paradigm denominations will still have a constructive role to play and need to adapt to this, not least by a more active learning from each other. This role will consist of the continuing functions of those denominations in the service of the churches and their particular witness or *charism* as regards their theology and practice. Thirdly, as far as the baptist or believers' church tradition is concerned, the most significant weakness in theology relates to a larger sense of the church catholic within which distinct congregations are to be nurtured. To rediscover this sense of being a relational, missionary movement is both theologically necessary and practically functional. It is for the health of churches that they know themselves to be part of a movement with shared

---

[7] Matthew 18:18–20.

convictions and values. In a so-called postdenominational world the more active provision of this dimension is one of the primary ways in which denominations will adapt to the new paradigm. With this in mind I now wish to return to the theological distinctives of the baptist tradition and argue for their viability in postmodern society.

The Vitality of Distinctives

Denominations have usually stood for some aspect or aspects of the total truth of Christianity that has or have been neglected by the wider church. They have often played a prophetic role, reminding the church of part of its legacy. I here advance the claim, which some might regard as pretentious, that a further reason why denominational boundaries have been being superceded is because *by default or design the church at large has begun to adopt values for which baptist Christians have historically stood*. It follows that if the reasons for holding a separate identity begin to be removed, then barriers and boundaries will be eroded and renegotiated.

I refer at this point to an article written by Martin Marty in 1983 that makes the point rather succinctly: 'Baptistification takes over'.[8] His argument was that across the board the churches have tended to assume baptistic positions. Similar points are made at even higher theological levels. Free churches are spoken of as the churches of the future.[9] Baptistification means still being Catholic, Anglican or Lutheran but in different ways. Marty is clearly not persuaded that this is a good thing, and if the process involves assuming baptist bad points we should sympathize with this judgement. However, overall it is hard to feel regretful that values for which one's own tradition has struggled have gained wider acceptance. It may help to pass some of these values in review.

---

[8] *Christianity Today*, 2 September 1983, 32–6.
[9] For further summary see Volf, *After Our Likeness*, 11–18.

For instance, we are hard put today to find Western church bodies that deny full *religious liberty* to the citizens of earth. It is a regrettable fact of post-Communist times that in Eastern Europe many of the traditionally established Orthodox churches are demonstrating an unreconstructed territorialism. Even in countries such as Belgium, France and Israel, threats to religious freedom exist at this present time. The argument has clearly not been won in all places and religious freedom is a commitment that needs to be explicitly reawakened, and advocated, in the spectrum of baptist convictions. However, church bodies that were once the very deniers of the liberty they sought now present themselves as though this is a human right for which they have always struggled. The Church of England and the Roman Catholic Church, explicitly since Vatican II, would now see themselves in the vanguard of those who work for religious liberty. If this is 'baptistification' it is long overdue.

Historically this is a shift for which Baptists can with integrity claim some credit. Although the granting of religious liberty has more than a little to do with the religiously sceptical values of the Enlightenment, these themselves owe something to the general trajectory of Protestant thought and to that tradition which goes back to the Anabaptists in the sixteenth and the Baptists at the beginning of the seventeenth centuries. It was here that the call for religious freedom was first of all articulated and advocated and this freedom, to worship and believe without let or hindrance, is surely the root of all the other freedoms we have come to enjoy. Coming from this tradition equips those who are in it to speak meaningfully and with integrity about the maintenance of this fundamental freedom and its protection against all ideologies, whether religious, anti-religious or irreligious. It is a fundamentally political voice. The fact that others have come to agree with us is an encouragement.

Related to this is the issue of *voluntarism*; the belief that religious acts derive their value from being freely chosen rather than compelled. It is always necessary at this point to distinguish the differing qualities of 'freedom'. From a Christian perspective, rooted in a recognition of human spiritual *inability*, we are not free to choose God: we *become* free when we are *set* free by the prevenient approach and grace of God. However, because this is God's work and God's work alone it cannot be prescribed or compelled by powers political or ecclesiastical. A commitment to religious liberty has as its corollary the belief that people and communities should be allowed space within which they may make their own responses, choices and decisions. Believers' baptism as part of participation in a believers' church has been the symbol of this in contrast with infant baptism, which is seen as overriding or omitting an aspect of baptism that is fundamental to its sacramental significance: personal response to and appropriation of divine grace through faith. A series of developments in a baptist direction are worth noting here, ranging from the critique of infant baptism by that towering Reformed theological genius Karl Barth,[10] to the advocacy of 'responsible baptism' by Jürgen Moltmann (also Reformed),[11] to the recognition in the ecumenical discussion document *Baptism, Eucharist and Ministry* that believers' baptism should be seen as the normative mode of baptism, to the widespread calls in the Church of England for the reform of infant baptism and even its abandonment. Indeed the *Alternative Service Book* of the Church of England makes provision for services of infant baptism *and* of child presentation, along the lines of the service of dedication and blessing used in Baptist circles. Parents may choose.

Once more, its commitment to voluntarism positions the baptist tradition well in a postmodern world that is so highly individualized that it rejects anybody's right to determine the direction of someone else's life. In explaining Baptist core

---

[10] *The Teaching of the Church Regarding Baptism* (London: SCM Press, 1948).

[11] *The Church in the Power of the Holy Spirit: A Contribution to Messianic Eschatology* (London: SCM Press, 1977), 240.

convictions it is often the case that believers' baptism is quickly understood by ordinary people to be coherent and appropriate. It may be objected that this is accommodation to the individualist spirit of the age. But there is an individualism that is inherent in original Christianity. Jesus called individuals to the decisive choice of discipleship. When stressing that the way to life is 'narrow'[12] he meant not least that only one can pass along it at a time. We enter the Kingdom of God one by one and not *en masse* or on someone else's ticket.

Out of the commitment to freedom and voluntarism comes the commitment to *evangelism*. If it cannot be taken for granted that people are born as believers (as with the older territorial churches) and if people must come to a place of decision and commitment on their own account, it follows that the primary role of the church is to bear witness to Christ in life and in word so that people may come to faith and be gathered into the church. Increasingly the churches of the West have abandoned the idea of belonging to a uniform Christendom in which all are Christians and in which the church's call is to be a pastoral church supporting from cradle to grave those who are already deemed to be in the faith. The concept of the missionary church has come to the fore, even in the European homelands of modern missionary societies and even in those churches that formerly saw mission as something that could only be done overseas. In this shift contemporary churches are once more following that already made several centuries ago when the baptist churches emerged out of the rejection of the Christendom assumption. It is to be noted that while Luther and Calvin and their followers rejected much in the medieval church they did not abandon the idea of Christendom or of the *corpus christianum*. As a consequence their missionary strategy was not aimed at converting the lost but at winning to their side those who controlled society, whether this be the prince (as in the case of Luther) or the town council (as in the case of Calvin). On the principle *cuius regio eius religio* (whoever ruled

---

[12] Matthew 7:14.

determined the religion of their territory), the strategy proceeded by imposition rather than persuasion. By contrast the Anabaptists, once they had embraced the believers' church and believers' baptism, and having rejected the notion that all of Europe was Christian, set out intentionally to win converts and to plant churches. They were enormously successful, despite the odds ranged against them. Their theological assumptions prepared them for their mission since they believed that the majority of people were not truly Christians and that their evangelism could not and should not rely upon secular power to make them so. They needed to hear the message, be persuaded by the Spirit of God and believe. Neither is it surprising that within the baptist traditions in particular there has been an enormous energy for mission, which has led to rapid church growth in many parts of the world, to the point that Christianity is now more a religion of the southern hemisphere than of the northern.

Within the contemporary world a resistance has grown up to the idea and the practice of evangelism that might seem to put those committed to it at a disadvantage. People do not wish to be 'preached to' and the idea that anybody has a monopoly on the truth has become more and more unacceptable to them. Strident voices, in particular the purveyors of religion, are often perceived as being in all probability corrupt, hypocritical, imperialistic and manipulative. It is this kind of reaction that we were responding to in speaking of the courage to be modest. On the other hand the baptist tradition gains credibility in the modern world for a number of reasons. It does not look for any privileged position in society but accords equal freedoms to other voices, simply asking for itself the same freedoms enjoyed by others. It recognizes that to be effective it must speak intelligently and persuasively to this generation and that it cannot rely upon capital accumulated from the past. Above all it relies upon the content of its message for its very survival and is not prepared for reasons of survival to take the position of a sect, a mystery religion, a new age therapy or an interest group. Its message is for everyone without favour towards colour, ethnicity, class, status or gender.

Here we can identify a further distinctive, that of *equality*. Although baptists within their congregations may honour those who hold office among them it is understood that those who so lead are drawn from among the people and are of one stuff with them. Their calling is to service among the people, not domination over them. It is therefore true that the baptist way of being church is a contributory factor in the emergence of democratic societies in which people are not treated unequally by virtue of caste, status or birth. Baptists are therefore unlikely to be people who show excessive deference or who are overly impressed by those who hold power. In societies that are deeply committed to such equality they are able to point to a history that has consistently stood for such a view.

A peculiarity of the baptist tradition has been to do with the *use and abuse of power*. It is under this heading that we may group a cluster of beliefs and practices that here come to the fore. While its commitment to religious liberty and its insistence upon the rights of individual conscience may be seen as a rejection of totalitarian government, this has been paralleled in the internal life of congregations by under-standings of how churches should be governed. The monar-chical rule of prince bishops was unambiguously rejected, its corruptions actual and potential being all too obvious. Similarly the oligarchical tendencies of Presbyterianism were rejected in favour of the self-government of each congregation. As noted, wrongly understood this is one of the potential weaknesses of the tradition, but rightly understood and practised, that is with due reference to the wider communion of churches that has spiritual and moral if not legal authority, it is also one of its great strengths. At its best, church government is exercised by the people, closest to their own situation and with maximum ownership of decisions made. Such flexibility grants church members a high degree of involvement in their own destinies. Properly understood although the outward form of such government is democratic its intention is *christocracy*, the rule of Christ who is head of the church.

Once more it is significant to note how within those churches against which the baptist tradition was a protest forms of government have undergone change. This is least clear in the Roman Catholic tradition, although even here there is a clear shift away from the prelacy and ultramontanism of pre-conciliar Catholicism with its focus upon the rule of the papacy towards the recognition of the pastoral authority of each bishop in his diocese, that authority emerging from the pastoral care of the churches. Within other traditions, the desire to play down the element of hierarchical rule in favour of values of mutuality and enabling has become the watchword.

In relation to wider society, it is a strength of the baptist tradition that we have pioneered and hatched some of the formative ideas and practices that have come to be part of our standard expectation in democratic societies. Whereas I would not wish to engage in the ideological eulogizing of democracy that goes on (even in democracies it basically comes down to the majority being ruled by a privileged minority), so far in organized human experience this is the least worst way we have found of doing things. Some of the credit for that must go to our own forerunners in the faith and this gives us the credibility to speak not only about personal salvation but to the powers of our day and of our world about what makes for good corporate and political existence.

Concluding Reflections

The point to which we have now come is one in which we can affirm that the values of this tradition are worth speaking and worth hearing in our contemporary world. It needs to be stressed that any reasons for sustaining a denominational identity of any kind should not be merely for form's sake or to preserve the past. As a recent publication asserts, 'A focus on the preservation of relics from the past or an exercise in mere denominationalism is the worst and dullest form of fundamentalism.'[13] However, to be able to speak both to the wider church and to the world out of a tradition that has been consistent, and out of a living community that to the best of its ability is seeking to live by the values of that tradition, is to speak with greater authority than if we were speaking only from ourselves and for ourselves. The voice has the greater authority because the content of our speech makes for human dignity and freedom. It has been said that a movement that does not have a past does not have a future. Those of us who are Baptist Christians have a past, and are drawn towards an even better future. Our past reaches back to Abraham and Moses, to Jesus and to Paul, to Luther and to Calvin, to Conrad Grebel and to Felix Manz, to John Smyth and Thomas Helwys, to Billy Graham and Martin Luther King. Because we stand in the living trajectory that arises from them we have things that are worth saying and that should be said. It may be in a postdenominational, postmodern and indeed post-Christian age that they are said. But they are worth saying. And they demand voices.

---

[13] Kidd (ed.), *Something to Declare* (Oxford: Whitley Publications, 1996), 54.

5

The Open Church

Many will recognize in the title to this chapter an echo of Jürgen Moltmann's small but influential book entitled *The Open Church*[1] first published in English in 1978. Of the many useful things Moltmann wrote in that work were his declarations first of all that 'the church stands or falls with the gathered congregation, the mature community, the open friendship of Jesus. This is why the scientifically trained theologian is, above all else, a member of this gathered congregation'[2] and 'There is nothing more urgent for the future of Christianity in the English-speaking world than to recover our "free church" and congregational traditions . . . The maturation of the congregation is the still open future of the Reformation.'[3] This is one of the points at which Moltmann explicitly aligns himself with the free church tradition along a trajectory already begun by Karl Barth. His larger book on the church, *The Church in the Power of the Spirit*,[4] is in my opinion the best 'baptist' book on the church available despite not having been written by a Baptist.

---

[1] London: SCM Press, 1978.

[2] Moltmann, *The Open Church*, 9.

[3] Moltmann, *The Open Church*, 15. Moltmann's language reflects the use of the German word *Gemeinde* to refer to the congregation as distinct from the world *Kirche*, usually used to denote the church but with more institutional overtones. *Gemeinde* is close to the English word 'fellowship' and the Greek *koinonia*.

[4] London: SCM Press, 1977, and 2nd edition 1992.

It would have to be said that the recovery of the free church tradition is not of itself the same thing as the recovery of the mature congregation. Those of us who stand in that tradition recognize that there is some considerable distance to travel before we can claim that our congregations have become mature. However, our commitment is to the priority of the congregation in the purpose of God as an expression at the local level of the church catholic. The mission in which we are engaged calls for missionary congregations, Christian communities that are shaped from top to bottom by the imperative of mission and orientated not towards the pastoral maintenance of the church, essential though this is, so much as to participation in God's saving purposes for the world. But this is true precisely because the mission is a congregational mission, centred upon the presence in the wider human community of Spirit-filled, Christ-centred communities in which Jesus Christ continues to take form in the affairs of God's human creatures. The maintenance of the effective congregation is therefore a crucial aspect of mission. Much of my own ministry has been spent in congregational ministry: the leadership and care of local communities of Christ's church. My conviction is that the upbuilding and sustaining of such communities is of paramount importance. But it is one of the most demanding and difficult tasks to fulfil with any degree of adequacy. These are challenging days for the congregation and its leaders.

The Strange World of the Congregation

Christians gather together in communities of worship, learning and fellowship. They have done this from the beginning so that congregational life is an essential aspect of their existence and practice. We might almost say with Karl Barth that the church exists in the act of its assembling together. Church happens when congregation gathers. When we are gathered by the Word proclaimed and around the

Word made flesh church exists. It is through such congregations that spiritual life has been mediated over the centuries to millions of people. The formation and existence of the thousands of congregations that have existed and do presently exist is a truly awe-inspiring aspect of Christianity. They are resilient in their capacity to survive, economic in their expending of effort, flexible in their adaptation to local conditions, productive in their ability to let people's gifts find expression and catalytic in their stimulation of wider social change. Of course, not all of this is true of every congregation all the time, but taken broadly and universally it is precisely true. The congregation or faith community is a marvellous invention. Supremely, these are voluntary, spiritual communities to which people choose to belong and in which week on week large amounts of sacrificial service takes place. Even when people do not continue in the faith, they can often be left permanently shaped by what they have gained from faith communities.

An encouraging development over recent years in the world of social and political thought has been the renewed focus on voluntary communities. So-called 'Communitarianism' has stressed the vital role that such communities play in 'civil society'. Situated between the coercive power of the state on the one hand and the individual on the other, they provide a fruitful intermediate zone between the two. It is in communities, of whatever kind, that individuals find themselves, since personhood is formed through relationship. Healthy persons are therefore the product of healthy communities. Where communities break down, with the concomitant personal havoc this wreaks, no amount of government finance or statutory assistance can fully repair the damage. Certainly the necessary support structures can act as helpful undergirding in maintaining or restoring community, but there remains that which money itself cannot buy and governments cannot provide. For this reason healthy intermediate communities are also valuable for the state. State systems are ill-equipped to do a host of things and so are best concentrating upon what they alone can do. Where there is a critical mass of community or family existence the burdens on the state, especially in its welfare function, are massively reduced. Politicians are wise when they recognize the limits of state power and use such powers as they have to support those voluntary and relational agencies that can deliver what the state cannot.

The congregation therefore is not only intrinsically valuable. Congregations are good for communities, providing places where people can be nurtured, supported, empowered and inspired by spiritual and ethical values for the wider well-being of society. They bring people together across the boundaries of age, ethnicity, culture and class in a common concern for each other and for God's world. They generate volunteers for social care projects. All this of course is to view things mainly from a social angle and it must be agreed that the social value of congregational life is immense. The decline in congregational life in the West is a tragedy for society as a whole, but one which society may not realize until it is too late. We could however explore further motifs. Christian faith communities subvert the idolatry of the 'powers' by coming together to confess Christ as the true Lord. They sustain an alternative reality to that which has the dominance in wider society. They engage in the dynamic of prayer, which opens up spiritual wellsprings in places where they have been stopped up. They help lift the atmosphere in places of oppression. By engaging in worship they gather around symbols, affirmations and experiences that inculcate the ability to resist and subvert the overwhelming power of what we have previously identified, with Brueggemann's help, as technological, military consumerism. Worship enables congregational members to pattern and centre their lives around the true Lord whose service brings perfect freedom. Maintaining healthy congregational life is crucial. This analysis helps pastors to identify both the importance and the measure of their task. Healthy congregational life is good for those who belong to those congregations and a significant contribution to the greater well-being of society. But there is no such thing as cost-free maintenance and those engaged in pastoral leadership are usually well acquainted with that cost.

Congregations and Family Theory

I have often wondered what kind of animal a congregation might be. On the one hand it is both like and unlike most other organizations. Take a business organization for instance. Congregations are similar in that they have a life that has to be managed and which achieves the maximum when they are managed efficiently. The larger the congregation the greater the need for systems and structures. Issues such as income, cashflow and viability are pertinent. Whereas economic reality lends a sharpness to business life however and a clear measure of success or failure, congregations are more diffuse, more holistic in their existence. They are profitable but they may not turn a profit. In turn this shapes the nature of leadership and expectations within the congregation. Because the decisions made and the programmes delivered are not primarily quantifiable in terms of a balance sheet or a bureaucratic function, leadership tasks are less clearly defined, more all-embracing and less supported by organizational systems and codes of practice. Ministers, quite rightly, are pastors before they are managers. Managerial skills are valuable acquisitions, but to reduce the pastoral task to management would be to distort it radically. The chief difference however consists in the fact that congregations are voluntary communities. They are dependent on gift work, not paid employment. Ministers may be paid, but they are unusual in that the church is primarily sustained by volunteers.

This simple economic fact is significant. How human beings behave will depend upon what is riding upon things. If I am in employment I expect that during certain hours demands can be made upon me and instructions issued, which I am bound to respond to if I wish to maintain my livelihood. Equally if I am an employer I expect my employees to comply with my instructions. In church however pastors are paid by the people over whom they have oversight. The employment contract is reversed, leading to high pressure that the paid professionals should deliver to the satisfaction of those who pay the salary. Conversely, because volunteers by definition are not paid, the degree of obligation they feel will be different in kind and degree from that of a paid employee. This does not mean it will be inferior – obligations freely embraced out of love and commitment could scarcely be described in this way. However, more often than not voluntary commitments will need to take second place to the obligations of paid employment.

If congregations are both like and unlike organizations, are they rather to be compared to families? The family is certainly an economic unit, and a very efficient one, but it is infinitely more. Through ties of blood, bonding and inheritance families are fundamental units within human community. Here we are born and nurtured and we learn the basic rules of interpersonal life. Acceptance of one another is not dependent upon economic contribution – it is a given. Yet families can be abusive. For some they can be places of terror. They can warp and distort. They can mark for life, for good or ill. Congregations are unlike families in that, although they will comprise many families, the primary bond that draws them together is spiritual rather than genetic or ethnic. We are brothers and sisters in Christ, but not in blood. It is easier to opt out of church than out of our birth families because the church is a voluntary rather than a biological association. However, because the church does resemble a family, and often will identify itself as such, people will bring into church communities their own experience of family life – once more, for good or ill.

Congregations, faith communities, are really quite distinctive, completely akin to neither organizations nor families. This said, of the two, congregations are more like families, it seems to me, than they are like organizations. They are not primarily economically determined, they are not highly regulated, they depend upon the choice to participate and, above all, they can be places of intense involvement and emotion. This is their glory, but it is also their potential dark side. People bring into congregational life their own personal history and formation. Family systems theory makes much of the ways in which we recapitulate in our future lives the kind of relationships we experienced in childhood. This is especially the case when it comes to ways of expressing and dealing with conflict. Families have different ways of coping – from denial through to all-out rows – that leave their mark indelibly upon us and shape how we might behave in conflict situations in the future.

One of the most revealing training events I have participated in was provided by the London Mennonite Centre and was concerned with precisely this issue – the ways in which congregations function as family systems. It was one of those occasions when someone, on this occasion Richard Blackburn of the Lombard Mennonite Peace Centre, was putting into words what I had many times experienced and never had the conceptual framework or the vocabulary to articulate. I began to realize precisely why congregational life can be so strangely demanding upon its pastors. A few gleanings are appropriate just here:

- Congregations, like families, tend to want things to remain the same; to maintain the existing equilibrium in church or family life. When things do change this creates anxiety and self-correcting mechanisms come into play to reassert the former equilibrium. Many pastors will be aware of the phenomenon of trouble suddenly brewing up and appearing as if from nowhere. This belongs, usually unconsciously, to the desire to keep things the same, to maintain stasis or equilibrium. Innovative pastors have to learn to cope with the emergence of the unexpected, and often the upsetting, as part of this. This can create an anxious state of foreboding along the lines of 'when you think things are going well, it's only because you are not in possession of all the information!'

- Pastors and leaders act as focal points for the transfer of displaced emotions. Experiences people may previously have had in their own families in relation to parental or authority figures, or indeed experiences from previous churches and their leaders, can be imported into new situations. Pastors can be blank screens on to which old movies are projected.

- In a parallel way pastors can become entangled in emotional triangles. When two people are in some degree of conflict with each other they can focus in upon a third person as a way of stabilizing their relationship with each other. Pastors are natural candidates for this role and can become ensnared particularly when they fail to keep an equal distance from each end of the triangle.

- Families and congregations have a tendency to load their anxiety on to individuals. A child for instance might be identified as a patient when the dysfunction is with the child's parents. The stress is simply surfacing in the child. Pastors might fall prey to a similar process as a less-than-healthy congregation unloads its symptoms on to its pastor. It takes perception to identify this and to disentangle reality and unreality.

- Pastors commonly feel as if they are overly burdened with the responsibility for congregational life – that they have to make up for the lack of contribution or responsibility of others. Consequently they overfunction, doing more for the congregation than is properly in its interests. Some pastors are driven to overfunction out of some unresolved agenda within themselves, the need to be needed, for instance. As a consequence the congregation adapts to the pastor's overfunctioning by underfunctioning and this compounds the cycle.

- Few pastors achieve what is a highly desirable quality in ministry, that of *non-anxious presence*. If congregations and families are the complex relational and emotional systems we have been describing then a primary skill required of its leaders is the skill of stepping down rather than stepping up the tension that is sometimes generated. Non-anxious presence is the capacity to control our own emotion and anxiety about situations and so to act as transformers that smooth out surges of tension and enable them to be controlled and handled. In place of our natural tendency to react almost reflexively to situations we need to master our anxiety to the point where we can bring solutions rather than further exacerbation into situations.

To identify these dynamics in congregations, dynamics many of which I recognize all too well, is the first step in knowing how to work with them. They explain to us why congregational life can become personally and emotionally fraught and why those in pastoral leadership have huge emotional demands made upon them from time to time. They also indicate that for those engaged in pastoral ministry attaining the higher reaches of pastoral skill and of congregational leadership requires extensive under-standing of ourselves and such self-differentiation that we are able to negotiate the complexities of congregational life. Of course, such dynamics are entirely normal in that they belong to the nature of congregations universally. Sometimes however, as with families, there are congregations where the dynamics become so askew that they become dysfunctional. This is where pastors might end up being casualties of the church's pathology. Churches that take this route need very specialist pastoral care such that few pastors are able to offer. Perhaps we should be developing new pastoral specialisms to do with rescuing churches from themselves.

What Makes for Health

The conference at the London Mennonite Centre helped me to discern the difference between healthy and unhealthy congregations. For instance:

- Healthy churches display unconditional love, whereas unhealthy ones make acceptance conditional on people toeing the line or earning favour.
- In healthy churches people are willing to assume shared responsibility for problems whereas in unhealthy ones people engage in blaming and shaming.
- Healthy churches accept people for who and what they are, whereas unhealthy ones engage in comparisons and competition, perhaps with other churches or previous pastors.
- Healthy churches expect problems and treat them as a normal part of church life, whereas unhealthy ones live in denial and delusion.
- Healthy churches accept consistent adequacy of people whereas unhealthy ones expect perfection.
- In healthy churches people identify and express their feelings whereas in unhealthy ones they are hidden and remain unexpressed.

Some of the pressure upon pastors derives simply enough from the fact that they are ministering in unhealthy churches. Often there will be an historic dimension to this in the sense that patterns of dysfunction are repeated within a church as problem people or problematic patterns of behaviour persist without being recognized, confronted and remedied. Pastors may be required to bear the emotion and anxiety of the 'system', producing the symptoms of which someone else, or something else, is the effective cause. By virtue of their position at the head of the community or organization they almost inevitably end up bearing in their own bodies the displaced anger and fear of an unhealthy congregation. At the least they will have transferred on to them emotions that have their origin in some other relationship or incident. At the worst they may be scapegoated and sacrificed for the sins of the church. I have occasionally wondered whether this is the kind of thing Paul had in mind when he spoke, daringly, of 'completing what is lacking in Christ's afflictions for the sake of his Body, that is, the church'.[5]

I have said enough to draw attention to the 'strange world' of the congregation and my purpose in so doing is not to highlight the improbability of congregations ever coming to maturity but rather to say that anyone who is making a relative success of congregational life is doing well. The complexities of congregational life are a reflection of that which is most valuable about them: their capacity to bring diverse people together in committed and engaging relationships that reflect the work of new creation in Christ. The integrity and authenticity of the entire Christian message is bound up with our ability to achieve such congregations on a regular basis. It is not that people are looking for congregations that are without a trace of human imperfection. Far from it. They would be intimidated by them. Rather they are seeking for congregations that through all their sheer human failings are none the less experiencing divine and human forgiveness and working co-operatively towards a better way. It is at this point that we can pick up the concept of the open church referred to in the title of this chapter.

Opening up the Church

Various practical approaches to church life are currently experiencing widespread exploration. They include:

- The *cell church model*, which locates effective church life in the organic principle of the small cell of up to twelve people as the fundamental building block of congregational life.
- The *purpose-driven church model*, which affirms the value of clearly structured church life deriving from a balanced set of purposes aimed at converting, maturing and equipping congregational members.

---

[5] Colossians 1:24.

- The *seeker-sensitive church model*, which aims at bridging the gap between church culture and the culture of the host community by means of creative and multimedia services designed for outsiders rather than insiders.

These models are not mutually exclusive nor do they claim to be the final panacea for the ills of the church. They are ways of doing church in contemporary society and have been applied with varying degrees of effectiveness in many different contexts. What each has in common is a commitment to an outward-looking perspective that fulfils the missionary imperative. In the cell church model this is expressed in the insistence that cell groups are orientated towards outreach, often in the 'household', the web of relationships extending out from the group. In the purpose-driven church model it is expressed in the model of concentric circles extending from the community beyond the church through to the crowd on its fringes, the congregation that gathers to worship, the committed who are its membership and the core who make it happen. In the seeker-sensitive model it comes through the orientation of the whole of church life and culture towards making it possible for outsiders to become insiders. In each there is a balance to be struck between those who are committed within the church and the openness of the church to those who are on or beyond its borders. This seems to me to be a fundamental aspect of effective congregational life: the capacity to build a committed membership while at the same time remaining radically and welcomingly open to those as yet beyond. I am tempted to say that it does not much matter which model is chosen to incarnate this principle. What is at stake is the reality expressed through the model.

For those in the believers' church tradition I suggest this requires an element of readjustment. Traditionally we have defined the church as the 'fellowship of believers' and have acknowledged one category of membership in that community: the membership of those who have committed themselves personally and sacramentally to Christ and have entered into the covenant of membership. However, the notional membership of a church and the lived corporate reality of the community of the church do have a tendency to grow apart to the point that one does not reflect the other. Furthermore, it is time to question whether the concept of the fellowship of believers really is adequate theologically to do justice to the church. Put baldly, if that is all the church is there is something lacking. Unless around the fellowship of those who believe there is a circle of those who would wish to believe, who are seeking to believe, then the church risks becoming an insular group of the self-indulgent and the self-preoccupied who have somewhat missed the point. The gathered church needs to be reconceived, and with a greater sense of dynamic, as the 'gathering' church,[6] both in the intransitive sense that it gathers to worship and in the transitive sense that gathers people into itself. In the subapostolic church those who had entered into the 'mysteries' of the church were surrounded by another group, the catechumenate who were learning to hear and to respond to the Gospel of Christ. The church therefore, although distinct and bounded, was also open to those whom the Spirit was drawing and incorporating into the wider community of the congregation.

In different ways the models of church we have reviewed are all working with this insight and derive from the belief that traditional models of church are not working. The effective church is the open church. To illuminate this further use is occasionally made of sociological models of church.[7] At one end of a spectrum is the 'closed set', the kind of church that draws a clear boundary between those who belong and those who do not by establishing demanding criteria for membership. At the other end is the 'centre set', which leaves the

---

[6] See on this Keith Jones, *A Believing Church* (Didcot, Oxford: Baptist Union, 1998), 38.

[7] As for instance by Anne Wilkinson-Hayes,'Notes in the Margin': *New Ways of being the Gathered Church* (Hertfordshire, UK: Hertfordshire Baptist Association, 1999), 12–15.

boundary between the ins and the outs undefined and untidy but maintains a clear central focus in the Lordship of Christ. It is not too difficult to think of churches that match these types – at one end the assembly of closed brethren that will not even share table fellowship with unbelievers; at the other the lively parish church whose services are available to all in the parish. Both models have their strengths in that one can build deeply committed and bonded communities whose people know about separation from the world and commitment to the cause, whereas the other can remain accessible and open to all comers. As portrayed these are of course two ends of a spectrum and most congregations will be located somewhere between the two ends.

Locating Baptist Church Life

Baptist churches can often be a combination of both models operating with a formal membership characteristic of one end of the spectrum (one single form of membership based upon distinct criteria to which you either belong or not), while in actuality existing as a worshipping community embracing all manner of people who are not in formal membership but who feel themselves to belong. Perhaps it is too predictable to suggest that a combination of models somewhere along the spectrum of possibilities is precisely what is required in order to gain from the advantages of each. However, whereas in most Baptist churches the models combine by default, unintentionally and relatively incoherently, an intentional combination could be attempted. In this primacy is given to the congregation that actually exists and in which there are various ways of belonging.

- Some belong as fully recognized church members having fulfilled all the stated criteria and having been formally embraced by the existing membership.
- Others belong as communicant members, not yet in formal

membership or happy to remain so, yet participating in the sacramental life of the church and held closely in fellowship.

- Some belong as the children of the church, growing into faith and as such part of the catechumenate and, if not members of the Body of Christ, certainly embraced by that Body and held as part of it.
- Others are part of the adult catechumenate, receiving instruction in the faith and in discipleship.
- Others still are seekers after God who have not yet come to a confession of personal faith but are travelling in that direction, perhaps through participation in Alpha or the equivalent.
- Some are receiving hospitality, either because they are temporary residents or because they are in a time of recovery or reorientation. They are unlikely to make it into formal membership but can find a home in the community of the church.
- Others belong to the church's fringe and yet it is from the fringe that new members are most likely to come and so a sense of belonging is appropriate and constructive.
- And perhaps there are more risky and tenuous forms of belonging – the extended belonging of unbelieving or no-longer believing family members, or of those who come within the pastoral care of the church in its widest sense, or of former members now disaffected and distant. Perhaps they still belong, but paradoxically without belonging.

In the actuality of church life congregations are composed of just such people as I have listed. Congregations rise and fall, they blow hot and cold, they fluctuate with the season, or the economy, they oscillate between intensity and apathy, they change from year to year and sometimes from month to month, they have comings and they have goings, births and deaths, joys and sorrows. They are organic and living, predictable and unpredictable. In the contemporary world they are threatened by demanding work patterns, by the consumerist culture that withholds commitment, by patterns of leisure that take priority, by mobility and fragmentation that open up diverse options and responsibilities. They need watching and tending, anticipating and enduring. Yet their survival and their health is vital.

Spirituality and Covenant

There are many ways of belonging to a community, but the congregation is a particular kind of community, a spiritual one and in our case a Christian one. Congregations do not endure and they do not thrive unless they are characterized by *covenant* – open-ended commitment to God and to each other in Christ. It is appropriate that we acknowledge the priority of the community and of the diverse ways of belonging. It is appropriate that we affirm and celebrate these differing ways of belonging. But the congregation is unlikely to endure unless as its core there are those who commit themselves on a *covenantal* basis. We may therefore distinguish two qualities of belonging – community membership, which is open to all, and covenanted membership, which is open to all who will accept its demands of time and commitment. The privileges (in a self-seeking sense) of such covenantal membership are few, but the responsibilities are considerable. Those who share in community membership have an open invitation to become part of the covenanted membership if they are willing to accept its demands. Covenanted members bear the responsibility of ensuring that church happens, that it is there and that it is resourced for its mission. They are the load-bearers, the ones who can be relied upon, the ones who have a mind not just for the benefits of the church but also for its government. They make church happen and they bequeath it to the next generation. They are the ones upon whom the maturation of the congregation will depend. Their value is beyond calculation.

It need hardly be said that the leadership of such congregations is a hard and demanding task that will entail joy and suffering in equal measure. Part of the pastoral vocation is the call to suffer on behalf of the church, to travail in giving birth. Perhaps if more of us understood this at the beginning the church would have fewer pastors! The reconciliation of church and world was accomplished by means of Christ's suffering. It is hard to imagine how in the pastoral vocation, which enters into and prolongs this redeeming work, it could ever be otherwise. Our discussion about congregations and their complexities reveals the fact that although the essentials of pastoral care may be few and simple – teaching people and caring for them in Christ – the skills it requires are considerable. It is emotionally highly demanding. It will stretch the most gifted to the limit when its demands are fully embraced.

6

Sustainable Evangelism

Of all Christians, Baptist Christians should understand that unless we evangelize we die. The practice of believers' baptism means that faith cannot be inherited – it can only be born anew in every generation. The concept of the 'gathering church' indicates that a primary aspect of the life of each congregation is that of gathering into community and into faith those who are being drawn by the Spirit of God into the life of God. The church of God is God's primary agent in proclaiming the good news of Jesus Christ and its aim is conversion – the turning of God's human creatures to God through Christ by the Spirit. It seeks to reproduce itself and to extend the circle of those who have responded to God's grace. When it loses the desire or the capacity to do this it is symptomatic of a deep malaise in the church's being. I agree with Sir John Seeley's claim: 'When the power of reclaiming the lost dies out of the Church, it ceases to be the Church. It may remain a useful institution, although it is more likely to become an immoral and mischievous one.'[1]

Transmitting the faith is of the essence of the church. If congregations are to be *missionary* in nature it is because the mission is essentially a *congregational* mission. Conversion is to do with being gathered into relationship with the Triune God who is communion. Salvation involves participating in the life

---

[1] Cited by Ernest A. Payne in *Freechurchmen – Repentant and Unrepentant* (London: Carey-Kingsgate Press, 1965), 11.

of God by means of the Spirit who draws people through Christ the mediator to the Father. The church exists as a community because first of all it participates in this communal life of God. Wherever it exists and wherever it relates to others it has the potential to draw them into this divine communion. As the Christian life is not a life of solitary individualism but of community belonging so the origins of the Christian life are to be found in those relationships with believing people by means of which we are drawn into faith and committed belonging. The ancient dictum 'outside the church there is no salvation' may have been misused over the years but it is in fact true.[2] The church is the means of drawing people into the relationship with God that saves. It does this by means of its community life interpreted and given force by its preaching and testimony. Through baptism and the Lord's supper it celebrates sacramental moments empowered by the Spirit to impart grace. At all costs we must avoid the idea that people come to faith apart from all of this. We must also resist the idea, propagated not least by Calvin, that the church comes along in second place to reinforce and support a faith that has been gained independently from it. The church is much more than a service station somewhere along the motorway of faith. Even when their search for God *begins* with some spiritual experience well beyond any contact with a Christian community it *leads* to engagement with the church of God. People are not won to faith in an individualistic vacuum – they are enabled to believe and to live as Christian believers by means of their engagement with the people of God under the influence of the Spirit of God. The church is essential in this very process, not a bolt-on extra. Take away relationships and there is not a great deal left.

---

[2] This does not prejudge the issue of the wider scope of salvation that may be hidden from our gaze but is known to God.

The New Evangelism

The train of theological thought followed here is clearly in line with recent thinking about the nature of evangelism in the contemporary world. This is sometimes referred to as the 'new evangelism'[3] and resonates clearly with the experience of most churches. At the risk of retreading well-worn ground it is worth indicating some of the main features of this approach.

For instance, the new evangelism reverses the assumption that people first of all come to believe in Christ, then amend their lives and then qualify to belong to the church. Instead they become attached to a Christian congregation in some way; through this participation they then learn how to see their lives differently and begin to practise a new way of living; then this issues in fully fledged believing. Believing, behaving, belonging (as in the 'old' evangelism) therefore becomes belonging, behaving, believing. Of course, an accurate observation of what usually does happen should not be made into an iron law about what always should happen. There are exceptions and variations. Yet the fundamental observation is an acute one. In reality of course the process is much more dynamic and interactive than this suggests but there is an insight here that rings true. Studies in the sociology of knowledge have revealed the extent to which our ways of knowing the world are determined by the group in which we participate. What is self-evident in one social context is anything but in many others. The 'plausibility structures' at work in various communities differ widely. Increasingly, in the secularized cultures predominant in the West any form of metaphysical or theological belief is swimming against the tide. To maintain a theological worldview as a public and open stance therefore requires a constant output of energy. This becomes difficult for individuals to maintain without a community that shares the same beliefs to support them. Some

---

[3] e.g. John Drane, *Evangelism for a New Age: Creating Churches for the Next Century* (London: Marshall Pickering, 1994).

only manage to survive in this climate by practising an 'enthusiastic dualism', which cheerfully keeps the different worlds in which they live apart and makes no attempt to relate them. To live as a believer therefore, and all the more to seek to make theological sense of the differing communities in which we live, requires participation in a community that can both nurture a Christian worldview and enable us to relate this to other communities in which it is not 'plausible'. For new Christians, the faith communities of the Christian movement are the means by which they are enabled to believe and drawn through the living relationships of the church into the communion of the Triune God.

This process takes time. It is not possible to count on people beyond the church having anything more than the most rudimentary knowledge of what Christians believe. The gap between church and dominant culture is growing wider and the Christian message (let alone odd bits of church culture) is incomprehensible to many. It takes time to cross the gap. The success of Alpha-type programmes in recent years is largely to do with recognizing that there is a journey that people need both time and an accepting environment to complete. Research into how people find faith makes it clear that the great majority of those who do so define the process as 'gradual' rather than sudden.[4] This is not surprising if coming to faith involves a process of osmosis, of slowly imbibing new ways of thinking, behaving and relating. Time, however, is not the only issue. There is also the matter of space – hospitable space within which people can explore and try out a new way of life, and in which they can ask questions and make lifestyle choices without fear of condemnation or rejection.

A further assumption concerns a shift from doctrine to spirituality. This is not to say that doctrine is unhelpful, only that it needs increasingly to be shown to have consequences for the way in which the Christian life is lived. People are

---

[4] John Finney, *Finding Faith Today: How does it Happen?* (Swindon, UK: Bible Society, 1992), 24–5.

rarely argued into faith by an intellectual system. They are usually drawn by a spirituality that first attracts and then persuades. The credibility and coherence of that spirituality is certainly an issue and people have every right (indeed a duty) no longer to go on believing something if it does not make any kind of sense. But increasingly people are suspicious of packaged answers that do not allow for anomalies and mystery. When they come to participate in a congregation they are rarely presented with a set of doctrines to be believed and most often with a demand upon the way life is to be lived, informed by the beliefs and values of the congregation. It is this spirituality that may or may not immediately impress them and only later that the doctrinal convictions on which it is based come to be explored.

A final insight to be displayed is the now well-established observation that the majority of new believers come to the church and to faith because of relationships of friendship and kinship. These two factors are the two largest single contributing factors to conversion. For many others who list something else as the main factor they constitute the largest single supporting factor.[5] Relationships supported by proclamation and teaching within a welcoming and hospitable community of faith are evangelistically potent. This is not simply a social or sociological comment: it is theologically rooted. Salvation is mediated by means of relationship with Christ through the Spirit and in turn finds expression in the relationships of the Christian community that lives within that communion. This is not to downplay the proclamation of the Gospel, simply to recognize the context in which it takes place. The Gospel is preached by people who are themselves connecting points with the church of Jesus Christ.

---

[5] Finney, *Finding Faith*, 38–49.

The Church as Evangelist

If the insights of the new evangelism are substantially
accurate, as I believe them to be, they are also replete with
implications for the churches. Churches that do not define
themselves as transmitting the faith clearly have theological
and spiritual problems of the first order. This is the primary
and crucial insight of the emphasis upon missionary
congregations.[6] Transmission of the faith is not an external
extra but an essential aspect of the lived worship and conduct
of the community. Through its relational life accompanied by
its proclamation the Gospel is passed on as others are included
and encouraged to pursue God. The ability to welcome
graciously those who are not yet 'behaving' as Christians and
to allow space and time for them to imbibe faith is a crucial
skill. It also requires programmes of instruction and education
to introduce people to the content of the Gospel and to enable
them to question it, and it them, in an exploratory way. To do
this properly means that church members (acknowledging
that not all will be equally gifted) must together be well versed
in the content of their faith and competent in the apologetic
task both of defending it from objections raised and of
applying it to the particular needs of individuals. This requires
skills of intelligent reflection rather than of dogmatic assertion.
Although explanation and argument have an important place
more important still is the ability to listen carefully and
respond generously, since the objective is not to win the
argument but to win the person.

It also ought to be evident that much church life as currently
organized militates against the church's task of transmitting
the faith. This is partly because the organization of worship
and fellowship caters for insiders rather than incomers, with
the result that people feel themselves to be excluded. But it is
also that the demands of maintaining participation in church

---

[6] Robert Warren, *Being Human, Being Church: Spirituality and Mission
in the Local Church* (London: Marshall Pickering, 1995).

life on top of work and family responsibilities allow the most committed Christians little time to develop friendships beyond the circle of church. Even when people pull back from church life there are many ways in which their time can legitimately be filled with good things, and so reduced involvement in church is no guarantee of greater time for evangelism related activity. When churches style their community life in such a way as to encourage their members to build relationships beyond and within the church this is most likely to shape the types of congregations that can transmit their faith most effectively. But part of the dynamic involved here is the ability to create churches that other people want to join. The question 'is your church worth joining?' is a salutary one. For anyone to wish to join a church, or even for a church member to want to invite someone along to it, the morale of that church must surely be at good levels. This is why renewal and evangelism can never be separated – renewal leads to evangelism and evangelism needs renewed churches into which to draw people with confidence. We need welcoming and affirming churches served by welcoming and attractive ministers.

The church exists within a dynamic of gathering and scattering. We gather to worship, learn and encourage. We scatter to witness and to serve. This is being salt and light. The light is intense and obvious; the salt is invisible and scarcely discernible. Both movements within this dynamic are crucial. Evangelism counts for little if there is no community base to sustain and nurture. Community counts for little if it is not extrovert and other-directed. For this reason each Christian community must apply itself to being an open church, welcoming of outsiders and able to assist them in their journey into faith and then journey onwards in faith. In doing this we need to value the skills of pastoral evangelism, that kind of evangelism with which most of our ministers are most familiar and which arises out of the week-on-week encounters with people in their homes or as they participate in church life. Other kinds of evangelism are radically handicapped without it.

Rediscovering Evangelists

Alongside pastoral evangelism, that absolutely necessary form of outreach carried out by the church in its interpersonal caring relationships, we need to revalue the work of the evangelist. Evangelists are people who go out beyond the boundaries of the church community into new and other realms with the message of Christ. The Baptist Union deserves credit for remodelling its understanding of ministry and its accreditation processes so as to take account, among other ministries, of the evangelist. There are varieties of ministry and calling and it is, on reflection, strange that we have wanted to make the category of pastor–teacher not just the dominant model but the only model with which we have worked. The move to a 'differentiated' ministry is appropriate and the recognition of evangelists is part of this. The assumptions on the basis of which this is done are important and here I set out some of my own. Before doing so, however, it is proper to insist that all ministry, including that of the pastor–teacher, is missionary ministry. Ministry is exercised in the service of the church's total mission. Even where someone is called to be a pastor she or he is also called to do the work of an evangelist,[7] and all teaching and preaching is directed towards turning people towards God, whether they be Christian or not-yet Christian.

My first assumption is that *we need many evangelists*. In fact I am tempted to say that we need more evangelists than we do pastors, precisely because the task is so great. The number of people outside the churches is vastly greater than those inside them. This is not to say that we shall ever get as many as we need but it does take us out of thinking that we need to accredit a few evangelists here and there. We require a whole movement of evangelists. Women and men, black and white, young and old, trendy and traditional: we need lots of these people and they must be as varied as the situations they have to reach are varied.

---

[7] 2 Timothy 4:5.

My second assumption is that *all evangelists need to be church related but not necessarily church based.* Evangelism properly understood is the process of initiating people into the Kingdom of God[8] and as such is a *polymorphous* activity. It takes a variety of essential forms, one of which is being incorporated into the Body of Christ as a member of the church. Evangelists who do not understand this do not understand their job. Even if it does not fall to them to be those who carefully tend the process of incorporation they need to have an eye to its being done and work with others to achieve it. There is abundant evidence suggesting that it is not that hard to lead people to make a first-time response to Christ; but it is much harder to build such a response into a lifetime of discipleship in fellowship with other disciples. But is conversion real and is this really initiation into the Kingdom of God if it is not followed through in this way? Evangelists need to understand the place of the church and to relate to it, but this does not of necessity mean that all will be part of the church-based staff team. Some will be, but by the nature of things will tend to be pastoral evangelists by gifting. Others will function at longer range or in more detached ways – but if they do so without reference to any local church, or a network of churches, and without its support and recognition, they can no longer claim to be church related and the nature of the evangelism they practise comes into question. If evangelists are servants of the church this service needs to be validated and recognized at the level of the local congregation.

My third assumption is that *we need to set evangelists free from the burden of overseeing churches.* Pastors can sometimes feel called into question by talk of a distinct category of evangelists, despite the fact that the New Testament itself requires it.[9] They ask, 'Am I not also an evangelist?' Since pastors also are missionary ministers called to 'do the work of an evangelist'

---

[8] For a development of this see W. J. Abraham, *The Logic of Evangelism* (London: Hodder and Stoughton, 1989).
[9] Acts 21:8; Ephesians 4:11.

this is a reasonable question. The answer must have to do with primary focus – maintaining the life of the church (which is an essential task) or being freed from this in order to reach beyond its boundaries. Put briefly, evangelists should generally be set free from having to run churches. Nor should being an evangelist be seen as a preliminary stage to becoming a pastor (although sometimes it might happen to be). Sustaining the life of the church can be a hugely absorbing task, as most pastors find to their cost. The pull is towards having so many legitimate ministry tasks within the congregation that the time and energy to be enterprising beyond it is in short supply. This to me is the crucial distinction between a new approach to evangelists and the role of the pastor–teacher (what other traditions sometimes call the 'presbyter'). Overseeing churches is such a time-consuming, energy-absorbing activity that if evangelists are to go beyond the boundaries of the church they are best not burdened with it (and it is a burden). Our denominational mindset might trip us up here, since in recognizing new ministries we are so keen that they should not be seen as 'second-rate' or as 'an easy way into ministry' that we might expect evangelists to do everything that pastors do – only more. But this is an unhelpful mindset – there are diversities of ministry that are to be seen as complementary to each other in the service of the church and Kingdom.

My fourth assumption is that *we need so many evangelists that we are unable to pay for them all*. Some evangelists will be supported financially by local churches, others by trusts, clusters, associations and Unions – but they will not be the majority. What we can pay for must not become a ceiling on how many we can recruit. Other accredited evangelists might be employed by 'parachurch' organizations. This is fine since parachurch organizations can often reach into places that churches cannot and have a degree of flexibility in doing so. The best parachurch organizations are careful to recognize their dependence upon the local church. Valuable experience gained in these organizations might later be harnessed within local churches as evangelists vary their ministries. The crucial point is that not being church based should not mean being unrelated to church.

Then there is the final assumption: *to be in Christian ministry as an evangelist does not mean of itself being paid in such a post.* Some ministers are financially supported and others not. Payment is not an essential component of ministerial recognition – it is incidental. People who have retired early are an increasing resource for the churches. Increasing numbers of people order their earning lives to set them free for other tasks. For some evangelists paid work will be something they do to accumulate the means to do what they most of all feel called to do. For yet others their paid or professional work will be an integral part of their evangelistic work as they understand it: serving and healing, creating and moulding, teaching and influencing, pursuing justice and fairness, creating wealth and well-being, expressing compassion or mercy. If evangelism includes evangelization of culture as well as of persons, a working or professional life can be an instrument of such a ministry.

The recovery of the office and calling of the evangelist is one of the challenges of the first decade of this millennium. But it must be seen in the context of forming a people of mission. Properly understood, evangelists exercise their ministry not as an alternative to the church being evangelistic but as a means of stimulating and enabling the whole church to fulfil its calling. Evangelism is not something that can be delegated to a gifted few. It is an expression of the whole being of the whole church. Evangelists are one way in which it comes to expression as the church sustains its enterprise in the service of God's Kingdom. This leads us to the question of sustainability.

Sustainability

I choose this word out of two convictions. Firstly, the work of evangelism needs to be sustained as a constant in the life of any congregation. This is not to say that it will always be pursued with equal intensity, nor is it to deny the value of seasons in the life of the church when it is pursued. It is to say that it is not a merely periodic activity that exists occasionally at the edges. It is part of our way of being, an object of our strategy, planning and budgeting. In fact, churches that can, and even those which think they cannot, do well to set money aside for this purpose and then ask how it can be used, rather than the other way round. Secondly, the kind of evangelism in which we engage needs to be within the grasp of the congregation and not pitched so far beyond them that it paralyses, discourages and demotivates.

It helps to sustain evangelism when we identify certain principles and allow people to relax into them. For instance, *evangelism begins when we exercise our witness.* Being a *witness* somehow feels more attainable for more people than being an *evangelist,* not surprisingly since all are called to be witnesses and only some to the office of evangelist. Witnessing has to do with how we live our lives in the sight of other people and how we interpret those lives when called upon to do so. Journeys to faith often begin with encounters with other people who 'have something different about them', whether that be a sense of purpose, or of tranquility or of quiet fulfilment. It continues when people are able to describe in a genuine and non-threatening way what it is they put their hope in and why it makes a difference to them. Nothing is more off-putting than bigotry and aggressiveness. Being an evangelist feels for many people to be beyond their capabilities but being a witness should feel to be within everybody's field of possibilities.

Secondly, *evangelism continues when we recognize that we all have a preferred style for exercising our witness.* For many people that style will have to do with serving people, caring for them in a time of need or simply showing acts of helpfulness and kindness as the opportunity provides. For others it will be relational, making connections with people and lending a listening ear, or perhaps professional, expressed through a job done excellently and graciously. Some others will express it through gifts of hospitality, inviting others into their homes, or through music that captures and interprets the life of faith. For yet others their style will be more intellectual, concerned with the worldviews that people assume and the beliefs by which they live. Rather than seek to be something we are not, the best is achieved when people are allowed to be what they are and to see in this both the gifting of God and the most natural and unforced way to exercise witness. This brings us to a further principle.

Evangelism gathers pace when we exercise our witness symphonically. As the instruments in an orchestra have different parts to play and yet contribute to a total creative performance, so along with other believers our own isolated parts gather strength when they are part of a greater whole. It is not up to us to seek to be all the instruments in the orchestra or to be any other instruments than the ones we are. The parts we play will differ. Most will get lost in the swell of the music. Some may occupy the limelight as they play crucial roles from time to time. But all are part of the orchestra and it would be weaker without each one. We may be hard put to keep to any other tune than the one we have to play, but orchestrated by a skilful director we can make a noise together to the glory of God and the benefit of those who hear.

A final principle is one that, in a variety of ways, we have already identified. *Evangelism takes place out of living communities of faith, which are indispensable to the evangelistic task.* It is for this reason, of course, that our churches should be worth joining. When we bear our witness there comes a point when we need somewhere to take people. Conversion includes incorporation into the people of God and it is as well that people should have the chance to encounter the people of God earlier rather than later. Seekers after God can then be drawn into the orbit of believers who are gifted in various ways to help them onwards in their journey. At this point the church at its best is a powerful converting dynamic, drawing people into a community life in which the sense of the presence of God can be impressive. Passionate spirituality is infectious and persuasive and churches that embody this will rarely lack new converts. Churches serve themselves well when they provide opportunities for those who are simply interested in faith to make connections with the very people who can help them.

Evangelism and Identity

It is intriguing that in the minimalist document that is the Baptist Union Declaration of Principle the final statement reads 'That it is the duty of every disciple to bear personal witness to the Gospel of Jesus Christ, and to take part in the evangelisation of the world'. This serves as a good summary statement for this chapter. It is also a reminder that for this evangelical denomination evangelism is a constitutive part of our identity. We are most truly ourselves when we are an evangelistic people, bearing witness to the truth and the salvation that are in Jesus Christ. Of all the mission imperatives that are laid upon us evangelism is at the top. The Baptist Union would serve itself and its churches well if at this early stage of a new millennium it were to turn its attention in a concentrated way to shaping an approach to evangelism that was an accurate expression of the way of being church we have embraced. If for some years at the close of the twentieth century we have spent time and energy rethinking and reforming our common life, it is crucial both to remember and to act upon the fact that it is all for the sake of our mission and calling as a witnessing people.

Within a large vision of what mission involves the renewal of our calling as an evangelical people would hold together the need for convinced evangelism and religious liberty, for individual witness and the centrality of the congregation, for spiritual rebirth and for its dramatic sign in baptism, for social regeneration and personal regeneration. On the basis of a coherent philosophy of evangelism it would then do well to design programmes, initiatives, training and resources that could be used by congregations, clusters and associations in the fulfilment of their task. In this way this body of churches would demonstrate itself to be proactive in the service of God and clear about its own identity and calling to fulfil its stated objective, amongst other things, 'To spread the Gospel of Christ by ministers and evangelists, by establishing Churches . . . And by such other methods as the Council shall determine.'[10] The call is not to an old-style campaign but to a reflective and theologically considered evangelistic lifestyle that can be sustained throughout the decade to come and beyond.

---

[10] *The Baptist Union Directory 2000 – 2001 – 2002*, 9.

7

Church and Society: Shifting Paradigms

Of all the challenges on our agenda for the twenty-first century the relationship of church to society and to state promises to require the most careful thought. One consequence of Christendom, the church's dominance in Western culture for over a thousand years, was to blur the distinction between the church and the world. After all, if the whole of the Western world was counted as Christian, its population having been baptized into the faith in infancy and being obliged to conform at least outwardly to the church's requirements, where was there any room for a distinction? The world had been baptized into the church, there was no room for a duality. As a consequence there was no room for mission, just for maintenance of the millennial state that had been achieved. Church and world were one and the same, church and state being merely different sides of the one coin, distinguished from another to be sure (most of the time at least, although with the edges often blurred), but batting for the same side. In such a world what was considered a sin could also be penalized as a crime and what was considered heretical, and so threatening to the well-being of both souls and bodies, could be punished as social deviance and dissent.

Christendom's vision of society has its own coherence and has left its mark in myriad ways on the architecture, the culture and the governmental systems of the world. It provided a unified and integrated vision of life, a social harmony in which all aspects of human experience could be integrated and catered for. It offered a sacred canopy within which life could be lived out. It is not surprising that some mourn its loss or fantasize about its recovery. It was not all bad and when compared with its alternatives or replacements there is much that could be said in favour of it. But the fact is that it has been lost and will never be recovered. Beginning with the Reformation Christendom became fractured beyond repair. Free Church Christians such as Baptists played their part in its breakdown with their insistence upon the right of personal interpretation and judgement, conscience and religious liberty and their desire to uncouple church and state, to unpick what had been extensively stitched together. They sought to restore the distinction between church and world, to insist that being a Christian was not a concomitant of natural birth but of new birth. Ethnicity and religion were not coterminous. Christian discipleship was something to be chosen and personally embraced – at a cost, not as an act of conformity. Partly as a result of these theological influences, but with other dominant contributions besides, we now live in a very different society characterized by the values of freedom, personal autonomy, individualism and self-fulfilment. To rehearse these values is to remind ourselves of the extent to which the form of Christianity the Free Churches espouse is both product of and contribution to the shape of our contemporary world. Despite the aspects of it we find troubling, Free Church Christians generally are reasonably at home in secular, liberal society.

Whatever the rights and wrongs of Christendom, and there are things to be said on both sides, it no longer provides the context of our mission. Yet it has been said with some justification that the church still tries to exist as a 'minority with a majority complex'; it still subliminally believes that this world is its world and its ideology the one that should determine the public realm. My concern in this chapter is to shift paradigms, that is, to explore what it might mean to acknowledge that we are now a minority in somebody else's world. To a large degree, this was the fundamental perception of that great missionary theologian Bishop Lesslie Newbigin, whose project on the Gospel and Our Culture[1] was premised on the belief that the church in the West exists in the same situation as the church in what we used to define as the 'mission field'. The only difference is that whereas in India the dominant worldview might be Hinduism, or in Japan Shintoism, in the West it is Enlightenment rationalism. Alternative modes of presence in this society are open to us once we have come to terms with a world in which Christianity no longer determines the public ideology. We are in effect a religious community to be compared with other minority religious communities in a multi-faith society, albeit still a large one with a lot of history on our side. Far from it being the case that Christians are in possession of the ideological ball and 'other religions' are trying to wrestle it from us on our territory, that ball is actually in the possession of another ideology altogether. The Christian relationship to faith traditions present in the same society is that we may discuss *among ourselves* what we make of them theologically, and we may discuss *with them* in order to understand them more completely, but we also *stand with them* over against the secularism of the public realm with a series of common interests and perceptions. First of all, however, we need to understand more clearly what it is we are emerging from. This involves exploring two understandings of Christendom, or of what is often called 'Constantinianism' – the alliance of the church with secular power.

Two Approaches to Christendom

I wish to distinguish between two forms of Constantinianism and in doing so to judge that one form is unacceptable while the other is not, and that both now belong to the past. In this I am speaking specifically about the Western experience and

---

[1] See supremely *The Gospel in a Pluralist Society* (London: SPCK, 1989).

predominantly about the English-speaking realms that are most familiar to us.

The first form of Constantinianism is the original one. From the Edict of Milan in AD 313 the Christian religion and church were progressively elevated over a period of centuries by Constantine, Theodosius, Justinian and other Christian Emperors to become the public ideology, the official religion to which dissent was not permitted. Inevitably therefore the laws of the Empire came increasingly to reflect a certain interpretation of Christian beliefs and assumptions thereby reinforcing the Christianization of the Empire. The crowning of Charlemagne as Holy Roman Emperor on 25 December AD 800 by Pope Leo III and the proclamation of the Holy Roman Empire represents the fulfilment of this process. So was born the *corpus christianum*: Christendom. Having come into being it endured for a thousand years.

The impact of this elevation upon the church was nothing short of a marked reversal of the countercultural and culturally deviant beliefs and practices of Jesus, the apostles and the early church. The dominance of Christianity was gradually achieved from the top down by the application of the totalitarian powers of the Empire. I have argued extensively in other places[2] that the total process set in train by Constantine represents, although it may have been hard to recognize at the time, a departure from essential and original Christian discipleship. This is evidenced by the way the church, having once been a persecuted and despised minority, was to become progressively a corrupt and persecuting power, directing its newly won might against Jews, dissenters and heretics. At the same time it arguably set a limit to the abuse of power in a way that other ideologies might have failed to do and created a beneficial inclination towards justice and mercy that

---

[2] *Disavowing Constantine: Mission, Church and the Social Order in the Theologies of John Howard Yoder and Jürgen Moltmann* (Carlisle, UK: Paternoster, 2000); *Power and Discipleship: Towards a Baptist Theology of the State* (Oxford: Whitley, 1996).

should not be overlooked. Even so, and even while recognizing that at the time of Constantine when the old religion was failing some kind of Christian response to the new situation was appropriate, from a radical baptist perspective Constantinianism in the form I have described cannot be legitimated. Christian mission today requires its specific and emphatic disavowal, or else the Gospel will remain tainted by the contamination of coercion.

The second form of Constantinianism functions differently. It too represents the dominance of Christianity within a culture. Yet in this case the dominance is achieved not by top-down imposition but by an upward pressure emanating from the grassroots and growing out of widespread personal commitment to Christ. In this regard it needs to be recognized that church, society and state are to be distinguished. However much they overlap and interact they represent distinct social realities. The state grows out of society and provides the hard edge, the coercive boundary required to preserve society in certain circumstances, and is the agent whereby society acts to achieve certain ends and goals. Where a society possesses a popular consensus about what constitutes the moral life this consensus will in the fullness of time and by a process of upward percolation shape legislation, which will in turn shape the executive functioning of the state. Where a democratic society gives its allegiance as a whole to the Christian faith the processes of democracy will ensure that to a greater or lesser degree Christian perspectives shape the organs of state. The obvious example of this is the United States of America, which has historically been a predominantly Christian society. In fact the form of Christianity that has shaped the USA has to a significant degree been the voluntarist tradition in which the separation of the powers of church and state (but not of church and society) and the guarantee of religious liberty have been paramount. In this context the separation of church and state is not the doctrine that church ought to have nothing to do with the state, but that the state has no mandate to govern in the realm of religious conviction or church polity. The church makes its impact upon the state by acting through its individual members who are citizens of the state and retain as such the right to bring their Christian convictions to bear upon the public realm.

It would seem to me that this second form of Christendom, if in fact it can be called that – and it sometimes is – is by no means unacceptable to those who stand in our tradition. It is often confused for the first kind with the consequence that its gradual erosion is welcomed as progress. Whereas I would always hesitate to call any state at any time a 'Christian' state, it seems to me beyond dispute that it is possible to have a *Christian-influenced* state and that this is a desirable thing – provided of course that the form of Christianity that does the influencing is one that is faithful to the way of Christ. The commitment to religious liberty is one useful touchstone in discerning the extent to which this is the case. There are forms of Christianity that, one suspects, would have it very much otherwise and, personally, I would fear their influence.

After Christendom

The point in making these distinctions is to say we have now entered an age in which both forms of Christendom have passed away. On the one hand the top-down arrangement that gave rulers supreme powers has been dismantled by the arrival of liberal democracy. This is not to be regretted. On the other hand the overwhelming Christian social consensus that made possible an upward moral pressure expressed though the organs of liberal democracy has also passed away, or at least has done so in certain visible respects (perhaps we underestimate the extent to which a secular and humanist worldview is also a stepchild of Christianity). This *is* to be regretted. The churches must therefore come to terms with the fact that the social consensus that determines the nature of the state we are in has in certain respects swung against them. It is not the case that the arguments have been won by other faith traditions. The dominant social consensus is now determined by secular liberalism, the prevailing orthodoxy, and no one faith tradition, nor even all faith traditions together, is able to determine the ruling social consensus, although they are still able to influence it.

The waning of this power to determine the social consensus is most evidently true in areas of personal morality. Shared societal commitment no longer prevails concerning certain moral issues that have consequently been marked out as areas for personal rather than social choice or preference. This is most prominently true in relation to divorce, abortion, Sunday observance and same-sex practice. Once the social consensus on such topics changes it then becomes virtually inevitable that legislation will follow to take account of what is actually happening within society and to produce laws that can be enforced without the law falling into disrepute. In turn legislation that in origin may have been viewed as unfortunate but necessary (on the principle of 'it is on account of your hardness of heart that Moses permitted this') comes to be seen as legitimizing certain kinds of behaviour ('it's legal so it must be OK'). A shifting moral consensus is therefore reinforced through the legal corpus.

Recognizing that there are differing Christian perspectives on some of the moral issues I have listed, I do want to point out that on many of them the churches have been seen to be on the losing end of the battle – guardians of the old order of a Christianized society rather than heralds of a Kingdom yet to come. Looking back over a century church leaders have battled against contraception, the liberalization of divorce, abortion, the removal of censorship, the decriminalization of homosexual acts between consenting adults in private, reform of legislation concerning Sunday trading, and the equalization of the age of consent for gay men. I have little doubt that before too long the church as a whole will fight and probably lose battles concerning the recognition in law of homosexual partnerships and the limited legislation of euthanasia.

Why is there a certain sense of inevitability about this

process? It is because liberal secularism is a very persuasive and coherent philosophy. It is founded on John Stuart Mill's principle that people should be free to do what they wish to do provided they are not infringing any other person's equal right to do what they wish to do. This social philosophy builds upon Enlightenment belief in the autonomous individual in control of his or her own destiny and assumes a plurality of religious, philosophical and moral positions within a population. If we are unlikely to agree about issues of 'private' morality, the best we can do is purchase the space for each person to make their own decisions according to their own conscience. It enables people to pursue their own beliefs and convictions without undue interference while seeking a commonly acceptable framework for holding together a diverse society. Given the kind of world we inhabit, which is not yet (it may have been noticed) the Kingdom of God, it is in fact a highly successful political position, persuasive to many Christians, not least those at the liberal end of Protestantism, and is the dominant model in our social life. As it has come into the ascendancy it has on the one hand displaced the view that a society might hold certain common commitments about the exercise of personal morality in favour of the recognition of personal preference. On the other it has also been accompanied, quite rightly, by a strengthening of our commitment to protect the individual from physical, psychological or sexual abuse at the hands of others.

Repositioning the Church

How are we to respond to all of this? My argument is that we need to shift paradigms – to reposition the church. The churches have regarded themselves as the guardians of a Christian heritage. As the Christian churches have shrunk over the last century and lost their influence the social and political position has changed dramatically. They have been watching the tide go out. Inevitably this has been dispiriting since there is much in the world we have lost that was worth preserving, and this is unlikely to be recovered. But it is dispiriting also because we have been used to dominance, to hegemony. We have assumed we are a majority when in reality we are now a minority and have yet to negotiate this passage. Underneath all we may feel there is the unnamed regret of our loss of power and significance and perhaps this is one source of the new appetite for political engagement. In so far as the churches have played the roles of guardians of the old values and resisters of change they have backed themselves into a corner. They have defined themselves as belonging to the *ancien régime*, the old order, unable to come to terms with the brave new world.

In all of this I do not deny that in much that has been said to defend the old there was great wisdom. Looking back it is all too easy to portray dissident voices as pompous fuddy-duddies standing in the way of progress. I suspect history will prove that the guardians of the old order were often right. In Britain in the 1960s, the legal action against D. H. Lawrence's *Lady Chatterley's Lover* appears farcical and profoundly ill-judged in retrospect, but it is a matter of record that the exponential growth of pornographic literature can be precisely dated to the judgement in that action. The Catholic hostility to artificial forms of birth control is unacceptable even to the great majority of Protestants, yet the detaching of sexual activity from the responsibilities of procreation has shifted seismically our society's approach to sexual behaviour.

Before attempting to outline a new paradigm for the church's mode of presence I wish to refer to the writings of the Chief Rabbi of the British Commonwealth, Dr Jonathan Sacks, whom I believe to be a very significant thinker for the Christian as well as the Jewish community, and specifically to refer to his distinction between covenant and contract.

Contract and Covenant

Dr Sacks sees the modern world as determined by two decisive traditions, one shaped by notions of contract and the other by understandings of covenant.[3] Modern society is based on a notional voluntary social contract between its various members. The contract requires members of society to fulfil certain mutual obligations out of the motives of self-interest and self-preservation. The obligations are minimal and preserve society from the anarchy or tyranny that might otherwise prevail. Liberal capitalist democracies, with their assumptions about individual freedom, autonomy and self-fulfilment have based themselves upon the philosophical fiction of such a contract freely entered into. The value of contract theory is that it purchases social space for people in a society where people disagree, allowing them a framework of freedom and security to live out their lives. Its weakness is that to function effectively and to allow society to continue at all, it relies upon the virtue of the people who occupy that space, upon their industry, goodwill and morality, their mutual commitments and faithfulness. Yet social contract has nothing to say about virtue and no way of encouraging it; it is an arrangement of convenience, a social construct and device.

This is where we turn to the concept of covenant, out of which, with its background in Calvinism, the notion of contract emerged as a secularized idea in the seventeenth century. Covenant has to do with unlimited mutual obligations and with disinterested love for others, the kind of love that is nurtured and expressed in families. It concerns itself with virtue. Covenant does not withdraw its faithfulness to another when a contract is not fulfilled. It endures. Covenant is nurtured in communities rather than societies (the distinction between *Gesellschaft* (society) and *Gemeinschaft*

---

[3] These ideas are developed in *Faith in the Future* (London: Darton, Longmann and Todd, 1995) and *The Politics of Hope* (London: Jonathan Cape, 1997).

(community) comes into play here) and is passed on by means of traditions, rituals and religious convictions within organic communities. Whereas liberal democracies are founded on the notion of contract, societies cannot be maintained without the reality of covenant. Contract societies fall apart if not sustained from below by covenant communities. This allows us a way of conceiving how religious communities might have their mode of presence within a plural, contract-based society.

There are resonances here with Amittai Etzioni's understanding of communitarianism[4] – an approach that has been expressed in a variety of political philosophies, left and right, and which I believe to be very fruitful. Effective states are dependent upon the intermediate and voluntary community networks that stand between the individual and the state itself. Religious communities and traditions fit into this category and so it is in the direct interests of the state to nurture and support these structures, not to threaten or undermine them, and to regulate them only in so far as is necessary. Out of this comes the language of partnership that is a marked feature of current civic thinking.

Towards a New Paradigm

The paradigm towards which we are moving is foreshadowed in the call of Jeremiah to the exiles in Babylon:

> Build houses and live in them; plant gardens and eat what they produce. Take wives and have sons and daughters; take wives for your sons, and give your daughters in marriage, that they may bear sons and daughters; multiply there, and do not decrease. But seek the welfare of the city where I have sent you into exile, and pray to the Lord on its behalf, for in its welfare you will find your welfare.[5]

---

[4] *The Spirit of Community: Rights, Responsibilities and the Communitarian Agenda* (London: HarperCollins, 1995).
[5] Jeremiah 29:5–7.

The situation of the exile, as has previously been mentioned, resembles in many ways that which faces us. We are in a kind of exile awaiting God's act of deliverance in the future. Yet this need not be a futile and unfruitful time, but one of renewal, rediscovery and grace after judgement. It is a time when we might discover more authentically our own identify. However, as with the Jewish exiles, there are adjustments to be made.

(1) We need to accept that the situation has changed. Secular liberalism has prevailed with its values of freedom, autonomy, individualism and self-fulfilment. Changes in legislation are the outcome of a shift in the social consensus and will result in changes to the law that many Christians might find regrettable. Christianity is no longer the dominant force in our society and needs to accept that it has been relegated to a secondary position. This puts it on a par with other religious minorities.

(2) This situation is not without its advantages. Supreme among them is that religious liberty is, at least in principle, safeguarded by the secular liberal paradigm and the church is free to publish its message without let or hindrance, as are all other religious groups. The United Nations Declaration of Human Rights makes this clear. Once we come to terms with the disadvantages of secular liberalism we might also see that it can be hospitable to dissenting movements, although it also has subtle ways of eroding them. The church is free to state its position as a minority group but will be most effective in doing so if it avoids giving the impression that it is in possession of the ball or that it speaks as something other than a minority tradition. The church should see itself as a 'modest witness'. Liberal democracy can be made to work for the cause of the Gospel.

(3) Accepting the new situation allows the churches to forge new alliances with other faith traditions. Along with them it is able to engage in a critique of liberal democracy and expose

the weaknesses in its versions of freedom, autonomy, individualism and self-fulfilment. For the Christian each of these values contains a partial truth and a potential error.

- Freedom is to be found in obedience to God, not apart from God; yet we have 'freedom' to resist God's legitimate claim.
- Humans are called to submit to God and to discover the true ground of their being by yielding up their freedom to God, not grasping it for themselves; yet this yielding up leads to a responsible stewardship of our lives in which we are more in control of ourselves than ever before.
- Human personhood is discovered in relationship with others, not apart from them; yet we are not wholly determined by other people in such a way as to lose our uniqueness and individuality.
- Fulfilment is found in losing ourselves for Christ's sake not seeking to preserve our misguided self-interests; yet we are responsible for actualizing our potential to the full.

Christians will benefit from hearing the cultural critique of other faith traditions and will wish both to make common cause at certain points and to resist those faith traditions at yet others, just as within Christianity there will be a contest between varying forms of conviction and practice. Secular liberalism can be hospitable but covenant communities will also need to resist its powerful encroachments in the areas I have indicated. The essence of this resistance will lie in the ability to recover our understanding of dissent, identity and community.

(4) Other faith traditions can offer us models of what mode of existence to adopt in a world where the prevailing ideology is not our own. In particular the Jewish communities offer both positive and negative examples of how to be faithful to a calling in an environment controlled by others and how to contribute constructively to that environment. John Howard Yoder once argued that the fall of the church took place not at

the time of Constantine but at the point at which the early church became estranged from its Jewish roots.[6] And the estrangement consisted not so much in a theological divergence as in a sociological one, a moving away from the minority existence of a distinctive people in a pagan and pluralist world. In many Western societies it is clear enough that Muslim communities know more about nurturing and sustaining a clear community identity than Christians do, and more about preserving the boundaries between their own community and the wider society.

(5) To acknowledge that Christianity need not offer a comprehensive legitimation for our society as it presently is is potentially liberating. It liberates us to be more specific and focused in our contribution, to be more faithfully Christian. Once more, Walter Brueggemann has wise words to offer us and demonstrates as he does so his own struggle to shift paradigms:

> It is tempting – certainly for this white, Western male – to view the new pluralism as a loss and a threat, and to wish for a more ordered circumstance of unacknowledged privilege. In my judgment, however, such a temptation should be resisted. It may well be that our pluralistic context of dispute and accommodation is one of liberation for those who assent to the testimony of the Bible. For in such a context, interpretive work does not have to bear the weight of the entire socioeconomic-political-moral-military establishment. It is possible that the testimony of Israel is to be seen, even in our own time, not as the dominant metanarrative that must give order and coherence across the full horizon of social reality, but as a subversive protest and as an alternative act of vision that invites criticism and transformation.[7]

---

[6]'Tertium Datur: Refocusing the Jewish-Christian Schism': An address to the Notre Dame Graduate Union, 23 October 1977, 8, 25, 37.

(6) To see ourselves as a minority movement in effect puts us back in the situation of the early church and aligns us more truly with the missionary context faced worldwide. These twin facts should assist us in rediscovering what it means to exist as a missionary movement that is only ever one generation away from extinction. The early church was concerned to pursue faithfulness to Christ in a world dominated by other powers, awaiting their overthrow in the coming of the Kingdom of God. This is our situation.

(7) Shifting paradigms enables us to move from viewing our present culture nostalgically, as one characterized (in Matthew Arnold's words) by the 'long withdrawing roar of the sea of faith', to viewing it adventurously as one still replete with the echoes of faith. Once we have come to terms with our minority status we are more able to greet as unexpected bonuses the ways in which inherited culture is shot through with the biblical narrative. Our world continues to be one in which the formative power of religious and biblical traditions is clearly evident and requires interpretation. The intellectual, institutional and indeed numerical influence of the churches continues to be formidable and to provide multitudes of opportunities for mission.

(8) Shifting paradigms does not mean ceasing to engage and influence our culture. It is not a strategy for sectarian withdrawal. Rather it points to alternative strategies of engagement and specifically to the need to exercise influence not from a position of inherited privilege but on the basis of merit, competence and intellectual coherence. The Old Testament in particular is full of examples of how this may be done, how on the basis of faithfulness to the God of Israel and the favour God shows it is possible to exercise constructive influence and 'power for well-being'[8] within a world that does

---

[7] *Theology of the Old Testament: Testimony, Dispute, Advocacy* (Minneapolis, Minnesota: Fortress Press, 1997), 713.

not belong to us. Joseph, Daniel, Esther and (supremely of course) Jesus offer such insights.

Jeremiah reminded the faith community in Babylon that they were exiles in a land they did not control. But he encouraged them to seek the welfare of the city and to find their own *shalom* within its welfare. Some might find this injunction tending too much towards the quietist and too little towards the prophetic. In a fuller picture we would of course wish to make room for both, and they are far from being mutually exclusive. A church that has gained the respect of its fellow citizens by its evident commitment to the commonwealth is more likely to be listened to when it finds there is something that just demands to be said. The years of exile were fruitful ones for the whole subsequent history of Judaism until this day and these years can be fruitful ones for us as we exercise our modest witness.

A final thought. We are living after Christendom. But to have a Christian vision for the social and political orders was never wrong. The church at the time of Constantine was right to offer what it could for the good of the social order. Along the way it was drawn into ways of acting that eroded its witness and its integrity. The challenge is to find a true vision, one that resonates with the Christ we follow, and to pursue it with intent. In my judgement the inspiration for this is now likely to come not from the powerful churches of the past but from those which have opted for nonconformity and freedom. They have always embraced, through their commitment to religious freedom, an implicit political theology that rather than legitimate the powers that be was prepared to stand out from them and keep itself free for the service of the Christ. In the changed situation what was once the position of some is now likely to become the position of most.

---

[8] Brueggemann, *Theology of the Old Testament*, 745.

What Kind of Ministers Do We Want?

It is inevitable as we consider an agenda for the church of
tomorrow that we pay some attention to the nature of Christian
ministry and leadership. If in this book we are concerned with
the identity of a particular Christian movement and believe that
a clear identity leads to confident and persuasive witness, the
same might be said of those who serve as ministers. If they are
confused about their identity they will be confused about their
work. In their understanding of ministry, British Baptists, who I
suspect are not untypical, appear to have moved from a
position of relative clarity on this subject to one of some
confusion. In the post-war period three major reports on the
subject of ministry were produced: *The Meaning and Practice of
Ordination Among Baptists* (1957), *The Doctrine of the Ministry*
(1961) and *Ministry Tomorrow* (1969). While differing, they
convey the impression of general clarity concerning areas of
agreement and disagreement amongst Baptists of the time.

Historic and Contemporary Dualities

In particular *The Doctrine of the Ministry* identifies an historic
duality in Baptist understandings corresponding roughly to
the General Baptist and Particular Baptist strands of the
tradition.[1] The earliest General Baptists limited the authority of

[1] Roger Hayden, *Baptist Union Documents 1948 – 1977* (London:
Baptist Historical Society, 1980), 29–33.

the minister to his (*sic*) own congregation; Particular Baptists were more open to such authority extending to other churches. As both streams of Baptist life became more conscious of the wider fellowship of churches understandings changed. Evidence of this is seen in the office of messenger, a translocal ministry (the world 'messenger' was a translation of 'apostle') that is to be found in its initial form in both groups in the 1650s. Towards the end of that century General Baptists began electing and ordaining messengers with a larger trust than one church. Among the Particulars, Daniel Turner in the 1750s stressed the concern of the churches for each other. This led to the practice of the minister from one church sharing in the ordination of one from another. However this progress towards a greater sense of communion and of the broader mandate of ministers was not uniform. John Gill, although sharing Turner's emphasis on the importance of the ministry, denied that ministers could act ministerially in any other church. This distinction has been an enduring issue ever since with Arthur Dakin's influential book *The Baptist View of the Church and Ministry* (1944)[2] strongly argued the case for the 'limited' or 'local' view. It is worth quoting from Dakin:

> A Baptist minister is one who is closely related to one Baptist church which has given him an invitation and over which he presides. He is a Baptist minister (with emphasis on the word 'Baptist') partly in virtue of that relationship, and if that relationship were entirely to cease, leaving him with no church over which to preside, he would for the time being cease to be a Baptist minister, just as a deacon ceases to be a Baptist deacon when he gives up the office. There is no sense in which a man can claim to be a Baptist minister when he is not the head of a Baptist church.[3]

Dakin's concern is to define the word 'minister' 'in such a way

---

[2] London: Kingsgate Press.

[3] Dakin, *The Baptist View*, 45.

as to make it clear that it designates an office in the church and not an "order" based on unique endowment'.[4] Accordingly, and consistently, college principals and tutors, superintendents, chaplains and padres are all to be denied the title of Baptist minister. Dakin was at pains to argue that this view is 'the Baptist view'. However, recent Baptist thinking does not seem to have followed him in this and in itself may point to a greater sense of the wider communion of churches to which we belong. In their service of ordination ministers are formally recognized as serving 'among churches of the Baptist faith and order' and it is expected that there will be wide representation at the service itself as a symbolic expression of this. Despite this it still seems to be the case that there is a structural fault line within Baptist thinking that is at least reminiscent of the historic duality which we have already noted. The theme of 'duality' will be a keynote in this chapter but it has become progressively less easy to categorize.

In 1994 The Doctrine and Worship Committee of the Baptist Union issued a discussion document entitled *Forms of Ministry Among Baptists: Towards an Understanding of Spiritual Leadership*.[5] The paper owed much to the thinking of Dr Paul Fiddes, who was its main author. It takes as its starting point what it discerns as 'two distinct views about the basis for particular forms of spiritual leadership in the Church'.[6] The first concerns what the report describes as a 'stable and underlying pattern of office', which is to be discerned both in the New Testament and in church history. Sometimes this pattern of office is seen in terms of bishop, elder (presbyter) and deacon. This threefold pattern of the Catholic tradition is echoed in the messenger, elder and deacon of the later General Baptists. Other Baptists have understood it as a two-fold office of elder and deacon with such roles as superintendents understood as extensions of the role of congregational elder or pastor. The

---

[4] Dakin, *The Baptist View*, 46.
[5] Didcot, Oxford: Baptist Union of Great Britain, 1994.
[6] Baptist Union, *Forms of Ministry*, 19.

language of those early Baptist confessions that acknowledge that 'a particular church consists of officers and members' reflects this sense of a given order. Since the beginning of Baptist life in Britain offices have been recognized by 'ordination', the word itself reflecting the idea of an 'ordinance' created by Christ for the health and good order of the churches.[7]

The second focal point concerns 'gifts and callings'. Rather than a pattern of office this approach begins its thinking with the gifts and callings bestowed by the Spirit upon the congregation and shapes structures and ministries out of them.[8] While valuing 'spiritual leadership' it sits loose to any specific pattern of office or given order. It continues a more recent Baptist suspicion of both the word and practice of 'ordination' out of anxiety that singling out such forms of ministry might suppress the ministry of the whole people of God. While valuing the teaching ministry this second approach may be more comfortable with the notion of a teaching elder as part of a team of elders than with that of an ordained office. It would certainly see itself as radically distinguished from the one-person ministry (and indeed one-man ministry) that characterized a previous generation of Baptist churches. It may stress a functional view of ministry that sees various ministries as tasks to be done by the appropriately gifted in the congregation rather than an ontological or office-based view more focused on the gift of certain persons for the well-being of the church.

It is worth pondering what has happened in the last forty years that may have contributed to the present situation. I identify two strands, which are not unrelated. Over this period Baptist churches have been strongly impacted by the charismatic movement. This has helped to bring about a much-needed shift towards the participation of the whole people of God in the work of ministry. The renewed emphasis upon the

---

[7] Baptist Union, *Forms of Ministry*, 19.

[8] Baptist Union, *Forms of Ministry*, 26.

Body of Christ in which we are all members and all gifted has been shaped by what it has rejected, namely the limitation of ministry to a state in which 'the minister ministers and the congregation congregates'. It is understandable that the rediscovery of the dynamic and charismatic has been accompanied by a critique of the institutional and the established. Secondly, in wider cultural terms Western societies have undergone certain political and social shifts that have left us less deferential towards authority, markedly more informal in personal behaviour, better educated than ever before and assertive of human equality over against hierarchical concepts and assumptions. While we are more tolerant of difference we believe ourselves to be less patient with suggestions that any might be 'superior' to others. As a consequence of these shifts, that are not (it must be stressed) without merit, our understanding of the nature of Christian ministry is left somewhat uncertain. And from this there follows for some ministers at least an existential uncertainty concerning the task to which they have been called. In uncertain times it is not to our advantage to have leaders who are uncertain as to who and what they are.

Persistent Sticking Points

Unfortunately, in discussing this subject it is not uncommon to find certain mantric utterances that appear with some frequency in this debate, from both ends of the new duality I have identified, that hinder its progress. Let me indicate some of them.

● *The priesthood of all believers*. Among Baptists this is a concept that has prestige and so to cite it is often regarded as the last word on a particular issue. It affirms that all believers have living access to God through Christ in the Spirit and so have a freedom and an authority of their own. It has functioned therefore as an antidote to forms of priestcraft and control that have discounted the participation of the whole people of God in the life and mind of Christ. For this reason Baptists have avoided using the word 'priest' to describe their leaders. However to affirm this shared priesthood does not mean or imply that therefore all are equally to be regarded as leaders within the church and that leadership becomes unnecessary. This is the intent with which this doctrine is sometimes cited. Indeed, all may share in the prophethood, priesthood and kingship of Christ and to affirm this is to make massive assertions concerning the nature of the church and to ground the shared nature of authority in the congregation. But Scripture is clear that some, and not all, are called to particular offices and ministries. Ephesians 4:11–12 ('The gifts he gave were that some would be apostles, some prophets, some evangelists, some pastors and teachers, to equip the saints for the work of ministry') and 1 Corinthians 12:28–9 ('And God has appointed in the church first apostles, second prophets, third teachers . . . Are all apostles? Are all prophets? Are all teachers?') give sufficient indication of this. The priesthood of all by no means excludes the calling of some to particular office and to leadership, since this is the way that those who are so called might make their particular contribution to the well-being of all in the priesthood of all believers.

● *The opposition of service and leadership.* Because Christ so clearly understood his mission as one of servanthood and taught his disciples that they were not above their master, it is often implied and sometimes explicitly stated that ministry should not be understood as leadership, indeed that the concept of leadership is itself in conflict with the idea of ministry, or service. 'Nobody leads. We just serve each other.' There is unease about any suggestion that we need leadership, let alone 'strong leadership'. It may very well be that the protest here is against secular models of the 'strong leader', and given the twentieth century's record in this area such instincts are well founded. Although the Bible freely uses the language of lordship and sovereignty it also subverts the very language that it uses by seeing as Lord the one who gave himself upon the Cross. It can hardly be denied that Christ, the pioneer of salvation, gave leadership to his disciples but in so doing he permanently redefined what spiritual leadership looks like. It does not involve domination and coercion but meekness and self-sacrifice. It can indeed overturn the tables in the Temple and confront the religious hypocrites but it achieves its ends ultimately by the way of the Cross. What is at stake here is not whether there should be leaders in the church but the content and style of that leadership. Christ-like leadership is not opposed to service; it is a form of service. It serves the church by offering something that is greatly needed, an example that points the way and leads into good pasture,[9] that nurtures and enables the whole people of God in their growth to fullness.[10] To deny the nature of Christian ministers as leaders is to ignore the development of a significant part of their work and of the skills they need to acquire. Furthermore where legitimate leadership is undermined or prevented it opens up the vacuum that permits illegitimate leadership to emerge.

- *Uncertainty about appropriate terms.* It might seem to follow from the previous point that I advocate a paradigm of ministry as spiritual leadership. Certainly I have struggled to understand what people are reacting against when they criticize leadership language. There has been a considerable vogue for the language of leadership and a corresponding suspicion of it. Indeed the terms 'spiritual leader' or 'pastoral leader' are sometimes used in preference to the term 'minister', which some hold to be an implicit denial that all God's people are ministers. Increasingly it is asserted that baptism is an ordination to ministry. In preference

---

[9] 1 Peter 5:1–4.
[10] Ephesians 4:11–16.

therefore to the term 'minister' the language of leadership has been chosen to designate those who fulfil particular offices. Are there unintended consequences to this? I have indicated my belief that to deny that ministers are leaders is to ignore an inevitable and necessary part of the pastoral office. People need to be equipped to be good leaders and given freedom to fulfil this ministry. This is not to say however that the leadership paradigm should dominate our description of ministry. The terms we use also have the effect of defining tasks and expectations. I suspect the choice of the term 'leader' unintentionally skews expectation in a 'managerial' direction. However, ministers are not primarily managers of organizations, or if they are they should not be. They are listeners to and bearers of the Word of God, they are theologians in residence and pastors of people. In churches where many church members are active participants and actors within corporate culture, the pressure is on ministers to fashion themselves in this same image. While acknowledging the crucial skills of leadership the language of 'ministry' remains more appropriate as the dominant paradigm for the task. Neither need it be felt that to call some 'ministers' denies the ministry of all. The New Testament itself does this in designating some as *diakonoi*. However, it remains a general term that is differentiated in the New Testament by other terms such as elder, presbyter, apostle, prophet, evangelist, pastor and teacher. It is unhelpful therefore if the word is restricted to the role of pastor (a tendency we noted in Dakin) but not allowed of others such as evangelists. There are varieties of service/ministry within which we locate pastors, evangelists and others.

- *Hesitation about the traditional term 'ministers of Word and Sacrament'.* The duality to which I have referred has sometimes been characterized as a tension between 'high Baptist' and 'low Baptist' tendencies. *The Doctrine of the Ministry* located the duality in an early difference between

General and Particular Baptists, *Forms of Ministry* in the tension between an underlying pattern of ministry and an emphasis on gift and calling. Now it is seen as a conflict between one gravitational pull towards Presbyterianism and another towards Anabaptism, in which Presbyterianism represents a high view of ministry with government and sacramental action located in the presbytery and Anabaptism a low view with authority and sacrament rooted in the congregation. We might on further inspecting the varieties of Anabaptism find this one to be less straightforward than it sounds. Undoubtedly some of the tensions in our understanding arise out of hostility towards the term 'minister of Word and Sacrament', which is suspected for several reasons. Firstly, it might be held to imply that the administration of the sacraments is the prerogative of the ordained. In so far as this position exists among Baptists (and I am not sure to what extent it does) 'low' Baptists would criticize it as tending towards a clerical, priestly domination of the life of the church. By contrast, the teaching of the Word and the sacraments or ordinances belong to the whole church and might properly be administered in principle by any member of the congregation even if in practice it is usually done through a pastor. The report *The Baptist Doctrine of the Church* (1948) captures this well when it affirms: 'It is the Church which preaches the Word and celebrates the sacraments, and it is the Church which, through pastoral oversight, feeds the flock and ministers to the world. It normally does these things through the person of its minister, but not solely through him.'[11] Secondly, there is hesitation concerning the word 'sacrament' lest it be understood that grace might automatically be conferred by the operation of the acts themselves. This is an issue we cannot afford (for various reasons!) to go further into at this point. The primary issue concerns the term 'minister of Word and Sacrament'. In a

---

[11] Hayden, *Baptist Union Documents*, 8.

wider sense those who are called to bear the Word, proclaiming and teaching it, must also have as part of their responsibility the duty of making sure that baptism and the Lord's Supper are indeed properly celebrated. As given, normative and norming practices they cannot be allowed to become sloppy or marginal to the life of the church. Potentially, any believer might administer them with the church's permission (Paul did not baptize all the converts in Corinth), but pastors and teachers have the responsibility to see them administered in a well-disciplined and wholesome way even if they rarely or never preside.

● *Distaste for hierarchy.* Baptists believe that the church exists where two or three come together in Christ's name and that the validity or competence of a local church does not depend on its relationship to an hierarchical structure, whether this be Anglican bishop or Restorationist apostle. But rejection of hierarchy and the belief that 'nobody is any better than anybody else' might also be hindering us from coming to terms with the reality of our own church life. All groups beyond a certain size create hierarchies, however flat and unobtrusive these may be, to manage their own affairs and activities. Authority is accorded to certain persons to act legitimately and with permission on behalf of the group and to have certain responsibilities towards that group. We cannot avoid therefore an element of superordination and subordination, and neither should we try to. We should rather establish healthy and accountable ways of managing power. A simple example of this would be a committee meeting presided over by a moderator or chairperson. For the purposes of the committee the moderator has authority to preside over the meeting. That authority is circumscribed by certain rules, written and unwritten, and could be taken away by the group itself if needed. But while it is operating the constructive committee member submits to the authority of the moderator and acknowledges that person's discretion and freedom to make judgements with which he or she may disagree. There is nothing demeaning about this in principle. In the church, congregations elect people to be 'over them' in this kind of way and it is no surprise that the New Testament writers not infrequently use the language of superordination and even of 'rule'. We should not be embarrassed by this, nor should we avoid using the language. But as we do so it is always understood 'in Christ', and as his own kingly rule has both subverted and renewed the language itself.

- *Concern about ordination.* Baptists have consistently ordained their ministers but in the nineteenth century there developed some suspicion of the practice among Baptists as part of their reaction to Anglo-Catholicism. Elements of this suspicion continue. Ordination would normally be understood as being set apart for a permanent, or at least enduring, office within the church. Because of its inferred (inferred, not implied) associations with priesthood, with the conferring of a sacramental power upon the one ordained and the suggestion that this marks a transition from the laity to the clergy, into a priestly caste separated in some ontological way from the rest of the people of God, some reject the practice and the terminology. However, none of these associations need be perceived as being necessarily implied in the term 'ordination'. Just as Baptists might celebrate communion (and even call it the eucharist) without thereby signing up to the doctrine of transubstantiation or practise baptism without embracing baptismal regeneration, so ordination can mean what our own theological reasoning leads it to mean. As the church ordains so it affirms and recognizes the call of God, according to individuals an authority to teach and to oversee God's people, which it believes God has already bestowed upon them as evidenced by their gifting, calling and holiness of life. Ordination does not as such alter who and what people are, other than in the highly significant fact that it may change the way they think about themselves, or the way in which they may be perceived by others. This is an act of legitimation, of authorization, so that ordained persons might know themselves to be formally commissioned as representatives of the people of God both within and beyond the congregation and the communion that has assented to that ordination. It could not be claimed that this is a necessary act such that a person could not be a minister without it, or such that the ordination 'takes' at a certain point in the ceremony such as after the ordination prayer or the laying on of hands. The minister who served without it would be as much a minister as anybody else. But it is a fitting and appropriate act that expresses in one moment what it has taken many moments to discern and to prepare for. It is tempting to say that a person so ordained is no different ontologically after the moment than before, neither do they become able to do any one thing that was previously inaccessible to them. However, in that the ordained person is set aside for ministry with the prayers of God's people those prayers must count for something. An endowment of the Spirit for ministry is surely our firm expectation and this must indeed mean a change. If we distance ourselves from the idea that people have something 'done' to them we ought none the less to look for a significant change in the sense that those ordained as an act of response to their call and ordination orientate themselves radically toward God for the fulfilment of that call and ordination.

Working with Duality

Having now identified and picked my way through these sticking points I need to gather the fragments and do something with them. In much that has been said there has been the sense that Baptists are wrestling with a duality. The exact nature of this duality has shifted. It began in my exposition as a duality of sphere: whether Baptist ministers are limited in their ministries to their churches or have a wider acceptance. It became a duality between the perception of an underlying pattern of ministry that is a given and the more immediate perception of the dynamic gifting and calling of God. It then moved to 'high' and 'low' views of ministry in what were perceived to be Presbyterian or Anabaptist tendencies. It could also be characterized as 'ontological' or 'functional' in nature with the emphasis falling either upon the fact that certain persons are given to the church, and the church does well to receive them and gather round them, or upon the work that needs to be done in the congregation that some are more or less gifted to fulfil. Yet a further duality would be between a 'classical' model with a high value accorded to 'given' ministries and a 'communal' model with the primacy being given to the congregation that needs to be variously served. Although the analysis changes there are sufficient underlying trends here for us to recognize the validity in both ends of the duality and to insist that it is in the combination of insights, most of which would be conceded by those working at the other end of the tension, that we shall discover the way forward.

To establish this point further, it is striking that both tendencies are able to appeal directly to the teaching of Jesus. The point can be made by referring to two passages in Matthew. In chapter ten Jesus appoints, authorizes and sends out the Twelve. They are integral to his mission and they go out as if they were Christ himself so that he can say 'Whoever welcomes you welcomes me, and whoever welcomes me welcomes the one who sent me.'[12] There is huge prestige attached to these words. To be sent out as Christ's representatives is to be as Christ himself. To receive these representatives is to receive Christ and through Christ to receive God himself. This is a high view of ministry. Contrast this with 'But you are not to be called rabbi, for you have one teacher, and you are all students [brothers]. And call no one your father on earth, for you have one Father – the one in

---

[12] Matthew 10:40.

heaven. Nor are you to be called instructors, for you have one instructor, the Messiah. The greatest among you will be your servant.'[13] Here is teaching that undermines hierarchy and patriarchy and excessive concern with position, prestige and prelacy and puts us all on the same level. All is swallowed up in a passion for God that overwhelms everything else. If we could succeed in combining these passages we might not be far from the Kingdom of God. The point is that the duality is rooted in Christ and that no solution will be adequate that fails to maintain the full tension.

Authority to Minister

My modest proposal for negotiating this duality involves choosing a lens through which to view it. It is the lens of authority, by which I mean not power but a weight of testimony. Those whose testimony is weighty are people of authority. All authority in heaven and earth is given to Christ since he is the true witness. Christ is present in the Word that is preached by those he sends and in the reception and propagation of the Word that is believed in the congregation. We have authority when our testimony is weighty and it is weighty to the extent that we bear the Word of God. Bearing the Word of God is the essence of ministry and is its defining core. Those who are called, gifted and sent by God to be bearers of his Word and who do so in the Spirit of Christ have an authority to minister that Word in his name. Equally, believing congregations that gather with Christ in the midst and under his lordship derive from his presence by the Spirit an authority to minister that Word to each other and to the world. The weight of testimony is at its greatest when both forms of authority come together, when some minister for the sake of the ministry of all and all minister alongside the some. In fact both forms of authority exist in mutual dependence.

---

[13] Matthew 23:8–11.

Although to be distinguished, they are not to be separated. In historical terms Christ sent out apostles who proclaimed the Word through which congregations were gathered. Here is the classical model. From those congregations others were gifted, raised up, tested, called and then sent to continue the process. Here is the communal model. Out of this dynamic the growth of the church has proceeded to the ends of the earth. Those who take a classical view of ministry would tend to stress the priority of the ministry before the church on the basis that the apostles pre-existed the church and were instruments of its coming into being through their preaching. This is why in Catholic traditions discussion of the church often becomes a discussion of the ministry. Those who stress a communal approach view the apostolic band as the church in embryo out of which the apostles emerged and point to the fact that all subsequent ministries have emerged from the church by the Spirit. This gives the church priority over its ministry. In reality this is no more resolvable than whether men have priority over women or women over men. As Paul says: 'In the Lord woman is not independent of man or man independent of woman. For just as woman came from man, so man comes through woman; but all things come from God.'[14] Those who are called to bear the Word need to be tested and confirmed in their ministry by the reception and recognition of churches or by a communion of churches if they are to avoid being self-appointed and unaccountable. Those churches that are isolated and self-sufficient need to open themselves to receive from the wider church those whom God is calling and sending as bearers of the Word for their benefit. To exist without this openness is to exist eccentrically. This does not mean that a church needs the presence of a minister to be a church, only that its authority, the weight of its testimony, will be lacking if it does not open itself to receive those whom God calls to bear the Word. In the same way ministers who do not mingle the Word they teach and proclaim with that which they find in the

---

[14] 1 Corinthians 11:11–12.

congregation are diminished in authority. The testimony of the church is most weighty when neither of these models is given theological priority over the other but both are affirmed, celebrated and maintained simultaneously.

Inclusive Representation

On the basis of this proposal I am now in a position to introduce the concept of 'inclusive representation' as a way of understanding the offices of ministry. Baptists would wish, I think, to reject the belief that ministers hold certain unique prerogatives, that is, that they alone can perform sacramental actions to the exclusion of anybody else. In principle, performing baptisms and presiding at the Lord's Supper may be undertaken by any believer provided they do this within the oversight and discipline of the local church. To deny this would be to fail to recognize the authority and the competence of the local Christian community, which should itself be seen as preacher of the Word, celebrator of the sacraments and feeder of the flock. Ministers may enhance, deepen and enrich this but not deny it. The understanding of ministry I advocate here may therefore be called 'inclusive' in the sense that the functions of ministers do not in principle exclude those of others and indeed that all members of the church are also representatives of it. On the other hand ministers should be seen as distinctively representative in a number of ways.

Firstly, they are representatives of Christ in that they have been called and sent by Christ. Although they function within and out from congregations, and indeed may only fruitfully exercise spiritual authority where this is willingly accorded, they are more than functionaries of the congregation required to do its bidding. They may be servants of the church, but the church is not their master. They are directly accountable to God[15] as well as accountable within the congregation. In

---

[15] Hebrews 13:17.

principle therefore a minister may find herself or himself set over against a congregation for the sake of the Word that they bear. This needs to be balanced of course with the opposite fact that in principle a congregation, which is itself the pillar and bulwark of the truth,[16] may set itself over against a minister if she or he wanders from the truth. The apostolic tradition is not carried on through ministers alone but through the whole life of the whole people of God.

Secondly, they are representatives of the wider church within the context of a local manifestation of the church. In their commitment to the presence of Christ in the local church, Baptist Christians have constantly underestimated the degree to which Christ is present in the whole church. As Christ bestows ministers and ministries upon the church it is upon the whole church that he does so. For this reason those who are recognized as being called to minister are more than simply ministers of one congregation – they belong to the whole church. For this reason they are tested and recognized in a wider sphere and instructed in the theological tradition of the church of God, in order that in the local they may represent the wider church and bring its wisdom to bear.[17] At the same time, by virtue of their recognition by the local church, ministers are empowered to represent that congregation in the counsels and concerns of the whole church.

Under this heading it is appropriate to return to the idea that part of Christ's gift to the church is what *Forms of Ministry* called 'an underlying pattern of office' to be discerned in the church as a whole. If this is the case, and I believe it is, what I have described as the 'authority' of local churches is maximized as they link into and benefit from this underlying pattern. The exact structure of this pattern is contested. Traditionally a three-fold pattern of office such as bishop, presbyter, deacon is discerned, or a two-fold pattern of elder (presbyter) and deacon. Other offices are seen as variations on

---

[16] 1 Timothy 3:15.
[17] 2 Timothy 2:1–2.

these themes. In more recent history a four- or five-fold pattern has had its advocates on the basis of the apostle, prophet, evangelist, and pastor/teacher (or pastor and teacher) of Ephesians 4:11–13. I remain persuaded that more reflection on these patterns would be of value, particularly concerning that continuing pattern of ministry that might be represented by the words 'apostle' and 'prophet', provided that we allow it to remain a flexible and porous pattern and avoid making it a stylized and ritualized form. That there are pastor/teachers and evangelists is not the last word about the shape of ministry as we exercise it.

Thirdly, ministers represent local churches to themselves. Ministers are sent in Christ's name and represent him as they bear the Word. They also represent the wider church in the local church and vice versa. Once received by a local community however and recognized in an office of oversight by the whole congregation they acquire the freedom to embody that congregation to itself because they now act in a representative capacity. They are empowered to speak to the church and from the church with an authority that exceeds that of other members. It is for this reason that although they do not exclusively administer the sacraments, they may consistently do so. As they preside from time to time at the representative events of the faith community they nurture the faith of the whole. A recent Mennonite publication goes so far as to use the image of incarnation at this point.[18] As ministers minister to their people they incarnate the love and the authority of both Christ and of the whole congregation, making present in bodily form the God who is with us and the Body of Christ in which we participate.

Status and Standing

The demands of both today and tomorrow require a robust doctrine of Christian ministry. I have attempted to offer this

---

[18] J. A. Esau (ed.), *Understanding Ministerial Leadership* (Elkhart, Indiana: Institute of Mennonite Studies, 1995), 24.

but not in such a way as to undermine the vision of the ministry of all God's people. These two realities are linked. The ministry of all will not be realized in its fullness without our recognition of the gifts that Christ has given to some; gifts that are in reality people being and doing particular things for the sake of the whole. There is a beneficial spiral of mutual interaction here. One sticking point I did not earlier identify concerns the rightful suspicion of any artificial and self-serving preoccupation with 'status'. Concern for status in ministry is bound to undermine our affirmation of the whole church by becoming overly conscious of the few. Sympathizing as I do with these instincts and sensing them to be well-rooted in the teaching of the 'Servant King', I none the less wish to stress the importance of God's chosen ministers being people of standing among us. If we accord them little standing, lest they begin to desire status, then we hinder the very ministries that we need. Status is what we seek for ourselves. Standing is what others give to us, most of all when we do not seek it. It is appropriate to honour those whom God calls and sends and as we do so to set them free to do God's work.

9

Baptist Identity and Human Sexuality

The discussion of same-sex orientation and practice has been one of the most painful experienced by the church over the last two decades. As a series of denominations in the Western world have sought to address this issue they have found themselves divided and conflict ridden as a consequence. Whereas a number of denominations in the United States of America and Australia have found ways of giving validation to same-sex practice within a limited set of circumstances, usually described as committed and faithful partnerships, those British denominations that have entered into the debate have found themselves so divided and uneasy on the issue that they have in effect settled back into traditional affirmations and by default or decision embraced the *status quo ante*. At the same time sufficient exposure has been given to the issue to enable active gay and lesbian Christians to organize themselves and make it increasingly likely that their presence in the denominations will be recognized and accepted, if not yet theologically validated. Although generally recognized to be conservative in their approach to personal ethics and so more reluctant to address contentious issues, Baptists also have faced these debates or will face them progressively. It is appropriate to ask therefore whether there are any distinctive Baptist perspectives on this issue, what they might be and how they might impact upon our own experience of this discussion.

The debate on same-sex relations is both symptomatic and representative. It is one of several issues of private morality in which contemporary society is at variance with biblical morality as that has been traditionally interpreted by Christians. The control of fertility through contraception, allied to a strong sense of personal autonomy that encourages people to negotiate their own sexual decisions, allied to a social liberalism that sees no point in interfering with matters that remain in the private realm and do not impinge upon the freedoms of others, has led to a major shift in sexual attitudes and behaviour. For Christians they lead to a tension between moral and pastoral theology. On the one hand there is the expectation that the churches will offer clear moral guidance. On the other hand, churches are also agencies of pastoral care in which empathy with people's needs is a high value. If churches hold back on the moral theology in order not to stigmatize individuals they are accused of not giving a lead. If they give a strong lead they are accused of being judgemental and of alienating the needy. How is it possible to do both? The issue of same-sex relationships is worth examining in its own right, but also as a case study of moral and pastoral existence in our changed world.

It is objected that it is unfair to single out this one topic for special discussion when there are many other topics that are of greater importance. Is this not an expression of the church's obsession with sex? The answer to this must be two-fold. Firstly, this topic has come up for particular discussion because there are influential lobby groups both beyond and within the Christian church that have campaigned intentionally to shift the consensus in this matter. If it has come on to the agenda it is because these lobby groups have put it there. Secondly, this is an issue that, once more, is tied up with the matter of identity. Instinctively many in the churches know that what is decided about this issue, in terms of church policy, will define for a generation the kind of church or denomination we intend to be. What is at stake is an understanding of what it means on the one hand to be a church that 'lives under the Word' and on the other to be open to those who are 'different' and inclusive in our practice of community. There are many who desire, of course, to be both these things, and just here is the challenge of this issue.

In this chapter I explore these topics from within the Baptist community. I shall be arguing that Baptist Christians will mirror and reflect those responses found in other parts of the church. However, distinctively Baptist perspectives may indeed affect the way in which Baptists handle differences of belief and judgement between them as it may also affect the way they advocate their views. At this point our traditional respect for individual conscience, the autonomy of the local church and the separation of church and state may shape our approach. However in addition to discussions of process we must touch significantly upon matters of content. We shall find it necessary to rehearse in summary form some of the positions taken in this debate.

As this discussion can raise the temperature to quite high levels, it may be helpful to indicate at this point that my own position on this topic is traditional and conservative. I remain unpersuaded and unconvinced by what I have read calling for a revision in Christian thinking. I will not be attempting to conceal my own position – in fact I shall be advocating it. While striving for fairness I am not overly confident that I, any more than others, will achieve it. At the same time I cannot claim that I have remained personally unaltered or unchallenged by the discussions as I have so far understood them. I struggle with the tension of how to hold fast to the teaching and how to be fair and generous in its application. Like others I have had to ask myself quite demanding questions about my own instincts, attitudes and commitments. By means of introduction I begin with several reflections on why this debate seems often to generate more heat than light.

More Heat than Light?

- We begin with the rather obvious observation that what is at stake in this debate is profoundly personal. When we speak of our sexual desires, instincts and aversions we are tapping into the roots of our personal and physical identity. Although we may approach the debate rationally and apparently objectively, it is not long before we encounter in ourselves some gutsy feelings one way or another about what is good and right. We need to face the fact that this is not a purely rational debate (but what is?) but one that for all of us will be rooted in strong feelings and energies.

- For those who stand in traditions that look to normative authorities in Scripture and/or in tradition the debate has become invested with a wider significance. It has come to be seen as benchmark or test of faithfulness to Scripture. The fear is that if we are able to shift position on this issue, there is no issue on which we might not conclude that the church has previously been mistaken and the Scriptures misleading. Indeed, approaches to sexuality are frequently among a bundle of concerns often seen together (I mention the reimaging of God as one other) in which what is felt to be at stake is the nature of the Christian faith itself. Those who affirm traditional positions on this question are likely to see themselves as struggling for faithfulness to Scripture and to the Christian tradition in general. Inevitably this produces great passion. To accommodate acceptance of same-sex relationships feels profoundly destabilizing both to Christianity and to society as we have understood it.

- On the other hand, those who want to revise Christian sexual ethics to accommodate certain kinds of same-sex behaviour understand themselves to be struggling in the cause of justice, the fair and equal treatment of individuals according to their given sexual orientation. They would be anxious to express that the church has been known to fight on the wrong side – in the case of slavery and the emancipation of women for instance – and that once more it has chosen the wrong side in resisting legitimate updating of its position. The paradigm here is justice, itself deemed to be a fundamental biblical concern. Those who affirm traditional positions are considered to be colluding in injustice and oppression. Although they may not themselves participate in acts of hatred and violence against gays, they are providing ammunition and support at long distance for those who do: 'If you are not for us you are against us.' Justice requires that the church change.

- We find ourselves straying here into a further field in which heat is generated. It is not long in this discussion before we encounter the phenomenon of rhetoric, the use of words, images and associations that are intended to undercut or disadvantage one's opponents in the debate. So, on the one hand, we quite quickly find use of the words 'homophobia' or 'homophobic' such that those who state their convictions against same-sex practice are deemed to be guilty of irrational hatred towards gays. On the other hand there is a ready association of homosexuals with paedophiles, with the insinuation that one is about as good as the other. There are, of course, valid points to be made about irrational hatred of gays and about the nature or prevalence of paedophilia, but it becomes impossible to discuss them on their own terms. The intention in such language is to hurt and to disempower, not to enlighten.

- A further area worth pointing to in these preliminary remarks concerns the sheer complexity of the issues associated with this discussion. The bundle of personal, pastoral, hermeneutical, theological and civil issues that comes to the fore around the subject of same-sex relationships is too complicated to be tackled through the blunt instrument of adversarial debate, which is the usual method of church or denominational councils. When it is so debated it is no surprise that both wisdom and time are lacking both to distinguish and to unravel the issues and work them through to any degree of conclusion. The debate exhausts the best of human energies and those who insist on prolonging it come to be seen as squabblers.

- Finally we indicate here the divergence to be seen in the relative concern shown between North and South, East and West. When the Lambeth Conference of Bishops in the

Anglican communion debated this issue, in addition to the concern to remain faithful to traditional understandings of Scripture, it was predominantly seen by those from Africa and Asia as a preoccupation of the wealthy, Western church. While in other parts of the world the ethical issues concerned hunger, healthcare and human survival, the Western church was consumed with inward-looking debates about same-sex relationships. This itself was seen as a profound and offensive affront to the great majority of human beings.

It is probably true that some of us are hesitant to enter this arena because of the emotion, and possibly vilification, that might be attached. As already indicated, for some the issue at stake involves faithfulness to Scripture; others fail to comprehend why there is such resistance to justice and equality. Whichever way, it is all profoundly emotionally freighted. For a church tradition such as our own that believes in a clear link between ethics and ecclesiology there is a profound challenge. Do we have the resources within our church councils at local, regional, national and international levels to debate this issue in a mature and responsible way? In theory this is precisely what our understanding of a discerning, hermeneutical community commits us to. Here we begin to encounter the issue of distinctively Baptist perspectives that we are committed to addressing. To approach these properly we need to approach them slowly. In the next section I address, albeit in summary and somewhat superficial form, the substance of this debate.

A Framework of Responses

How Baptists respond to the content of this debate is unlikely to differ significantly in outline from the responses of other Christians. I suggest that the following positions are all to be found among Baptists, although I have no doubt that some of them are majority views and others those of a distinct minority. I intend here to follow James Nelson, who helpfully and concisely identifies four consistent Christian responses to same-sex attraction and relationships.[1] Whereas I owe the framework to Nelson, the way I elaborate these positions and summarize them goes beyond his own description and therefore his own responsibility for them. Nelson identifies what he calls:

- The *rejecting–punitive position*. In this response homosexual orientation and practice are unconditionally rejected as being corrupt and sinful, in no way capable of Christian or theological validation other than as sin. Furthermore this position is accompanied by a punitive attitude towards lesbians and gay men, both in projecting stereotypes upon them and in seeking to penalize or discriminate against them in the civil realm. Homosexual behaviour is regarded as undermining and eroding the social and moral fabric of society. As a consequence those who feel themselves to be homosexual find it difficult to be open and honest about it and live in fear of ostracism or penalty. Homosexuals are presented with stark decisions in relation to Christianity – to reject it, adopt a covert lifestyle within it or stand out against it as hostile to their interests and identity.

- The *rejecting–non-punitive position*. Advocates of this position might rather describe it as 'rejecting–compassionate'. Homosexual acts are rejected as violating the divine intention but a distinction is drawn between orientation and acts. The divine intention set out in Genesis and in the teaching of Jesus centres on the complementary nature of the male–female partnership on both the physical and spiritual levels. Homosexual acts are rejected as irregular

---

[1] J. B. Nelson, 'Homosexuality', in John Macquarrie and James Childress (eds), *A New Dictionary of Christian Ethics* (London: SCM Press, 1986), 271–4.

and unnatural both when judged against this benchmark and when looked at from a simple physical perspective. Anal intercourse can find no biblical or theological legitimation. Negatively, whenever the Bible refers to same-sex acts it does so to condemn them. Positively, the only form of sexual behaviour that is affirmed is heterosexual. Homosexual acts are never held up for admiration or acceptance. However, homosexual orientation is seen as a flaw rather than a sin, as a consequence of the profound disorder in which we all share, whether heterosexual or homosexual. For this reason homosexual persons are to be treated compassionately as they wrestle with this disorder and given all assistance to overcome or come to terms with their particular struggle. This is the kind of grace and mercy we all need and so no discrimination should be made against homosexuals as a class of people within the church. The call to live a godly life is one that comes to all of us and poses its own challenges to each of us in distinctive ways. In terms of civil and criminal legislation those espousing this position might support legislation that was directed against propagating homosexual lifestyles or oppose legislation that treated homosexual partnerships as equivalent to marriage. In that the very continuance of the human race depends upon heterosexual marriage this must be privileged within society and by the state.

- The *position of qualified acceptance*. This position agrees with the two former headings in affirming that God's intent in creation is heterosexual in nature. God made humankind as male and female and commanded them to be fruitful and multiply. Marriage provides the basis for the continuance of society both as the context for reproduction and for nurture and personal growth. Heterosexual and homosexual partnerships can never therefore be regarded as equivalent or equal. If we were to universalize and ask what kind of world this would be if all were committed to heterosexual and faithful marriage, the answer would be 'a better one'. If all were to engage in homosexual partnerships, the answer would be 'a non-existent one'. Clearly, these forms of sexual behaviour are not equivalent. However, we do not live in a perfect or ideal world but in a broken and distorted one. Human bondage to sin should excite not our condemnation but our compassion. In such a world people are often faced with situations they cannot change and with choices that are highly ambiguous. Often they are asked to choose not between good and evil but between the bad and the worse. This is a principle that informs various areas of Christian ethical debate, not least our approach to war. All Christians would agree that war is evil, that participation in killing renders us guilty before God. Extreme pacifists have argued that under no conceivable circumstance ought one to participate in war and killing. But most Christians have argued that such a purist position is not possible in the kind of world in which we share. Criteria have been devised not to validate war and make it right but to identify the conditions under which Christians might participate in that which, though wrong, is apparently necessary or inevitable. In a somewhat analogous way, those who find themselves homosexual in constitution, whether through genetic conditioning or early nurture or both, need to be supported in their struggle to live holy lives. It may be that for some reorientation of their sexuality is possible and can be made to work. It may be that for others the gift of celibacy is given. But for yet others reorientation may not work and celibacy might prove to be a counsel of perfection and is not given to them. Could it then be that faithful same-sex relationships may be the least worst option open to some people in an imperfect and unredeemed world? And would this not be infinitely preferable to promiscuity? And is it not part of the church's responsibility to help those who feel themselves to be what they are to live with a high degree of ethical discrimination? Whereas there is nothing in my reading either of Scripture or of the Christian tradition to give theological validation to same-sex relationships, might it not be possible to draw upon the Christian tradition's understandings of marriage as faithful and enduring partnership to inform how responsible homosexual persons might make ethical judgements? Those who adopt this position of qualified acceptance would in all likelihood hesitate to ordain practising homosexuals to the pastoral office on the basis that this is an exemplary role and those who occupy it should exemplify as best they are able normative ethical behaviour. Whereas the logic of the position resists accepting gay partnerships as having equal status with marriages, it does not preclude there being some way of recognizing in law the value of faithful and abiding partnerships and undergirding them with such support as the state can bring.

● The *position of full acceptance*. According to this position sexual relationships should be evaluated according to their 'unitive' rather than their 'procreative' purpose. Sexual acts are not primarily a means of reproduction but of human bonding. All sexual acts are tested ethically according to their relational qualities. The same criteria apply therefore to heterosexual and homosexual behaviour. In so far as sexual activity promotes bonding, it is good. The ethical debate is not essentially about who has sex with whom but how sex promotes and sustains love between persons. In this sense same-sex activity that is loving can be infinitely superior to exploitative heterosexual behaviour. This position does not commit people to a sexual free-for-all. It is essential that sex express values of mutuality rather than selfishness, partnership rather than domination, giving rather than greed, commitment rather than promiscuity. All of these values are deeply Christian and a true understanding of the Christian revelation would see that this is indeed the tendency of Scripture. Re-examined and re-exegeted those passages of Scripture that condemn same-sex practice are condemning behaviours that the responsible and Christian gay person would also wish to condemn, whether this be the gang rape of Sodom, or the male prostitutes of Canaanite religion or the exploitative pederasty of the Greeks and Romans. Indeed, once carefully examined the Bible is found not to be addressing at all the issue of loving and faithful same-sex relations but forms of sexual activity that all sides of this debate can agree to be unacceptable. What the Bible might have said had it been able in its world to envisage the same-sex relations that are now being recognized remains a matter of speculation, speculation that we must turn to the broader themes of Scripture to answer: themes such as love, faithfulness, compassion. To recognize this should lead to equal treatment for gay people in the church, expressed in the blessing of same-sex unions and the ordination of practising but faithful gays and lesbians as well as full civil equality. Indeed, the church should have a concern most of all for the marginalized and the vulnerable and should be in the forefront of such a struggle. At the same time, the gay communities need the church's ethical guidance just as much as heterosexuals do. It is worth noting that although this position is the most liberal of those we have outlined, even here there is the characteristic Christian restriction of sexual activity to faithful relationships. It does not represent a sexual and permissive free-for-all.

Some Evaluations

The effect of outlining this framework is to demonstrate that there is not one simple response to the question of homosexual practice. Rather, there is a field of responses. Although I have followed Nelson in identifying four types, there is room for some manoeuvre between the types such that actual responses will be more complex than even they suggest. My judgement of the British Baptist scene would be that all these positions are represented in our churches, although not in equal measure. The considered minds of most churches would at an educated guess predominantly affirm the second position. But practical pastoral and civil involvement and realism in these areas would lead to some oscillation towards the third position.

Indeed, it is the interaction between the second and third positions that seems to me to allow scope for a fruitful conversation. I personally would reject both positions one and four. In the case of position one this would be on the grounds that it fails to have sympathy for people in the way that is properly Christian. Admittedly there are few Christians who would put themselves in the category of being 'punitive', but even so Nelson is right to discern that it is an observable position. Position four is also, in my view, inadequately Christian, in the doctrinal sense. Whereas re-exegeting the biblical texts that bear upon this issue certainly has shed light on what those texts mean and in some cases leads to a rereading of them, this seems to me to leave the basic issue unchanged. What revisionists must contend with is not four relatively isolated texts that prohibit, but a whole biblical witness to human sexuality that permits and affirms. But what it permits, affirms and leads us to admire is the vision of male and female in the complementary and productive union for which their bodies equip and prepare them. No other vision is offered. We are fundamentally engineered for reproduction and Scripture bears testimony to that which our bodies confirm. However, I am all too acutely aware that pastoral practice is often concerned with enabling people to choose the least worst options for their lives and to live with the reality given to them in which there is not always room for change.

This would be true for instance of divorce. My public position is one of the affirmation of marriage as lifelong and faithful union between one man and one woman. But my pastoral practice would allow for divorce and remarriage since as a matter of given fact we are often faced with broken and messy situations that we are called upon to repair and redeem to the limits of our capacity. We call people to live with and to improve upon their situation. I do not see it as my task to advise people to divorce, but if this is the decision they take I must often work with them to make the best of what is inevitable. I advocate marriage but I deal with divorce. If I were to advocate divorce I would risk undermining marriage. We live in the realm of the penultimate, not of the ultimate, and we live by grace. I confess therefore that whereas I have always sought to live and work as a theologically principled pastor I have not infrequently found that being pragmatic is necessary to see people through in ambiguous and uncertain times. So in the case of same-sex relationships to take the second position as a stance of principle does not for me preclude some oscillation towards the third position either as a pastoral approach within the church or as a way of addressing the civil realm in which laws and practices need to be framed to take account of many things of which personally I might disapprove. Let me come then to reflections on some of the issues of process this matter raises for us.

Reflections on a Baptist Approach

As already indicated, Baptist attitudes to homosexuality are unlikely to differ markedly from those of the wider Christian community. However there are several concerns which are of particular note for Baptists. As a people who have stood for the rights of individual conscience, to what extent do we allow for the conscientious disagreement and dissent of the individuals who comprise our churches on this matter? As we believe in the autonomy of the local church, to what extent are we content for churches to hold different views and what does this do to our fellowship? Conversely, in that we also believe that the discerning community exists in councils, associations and assemblies, to what extent are we content to allow there to be a regional and a national policy and what do we do when we dissent from such a policy? Finally, as those who have believed historically in the separation of church and state, to what extent do we distinguish between what voluntary communities of Christians may embrace as their own ethic and the need of the state to allow for and regulate acts or lifestyles

Christians might find unacceptable? If not uniquely Baptist this complex of questions is at least characteristically so.

(1) The place of individual conscience

I have not hidden my own perspective. How, then, do I come to terms with the fact that others see things differently? Historically Baptists have embraced a doctrine of soul competence or freedom and have had a high respect for individual ethical judgement. They can respect the consciences of others even if they do not share the same scruples or the same freedoms. Inevitably this has led to a degree of latitude as to how the Bible might be applied in some matters. By illustration, within a Baptist congregation there may be those who are conscientious pacifists, others who are 'just warriors' and might participate in war under certain circumstances, others yet who are 'nuclear pacifists' who might participate in a just war but could not support nuclear war or preparation for it. We are used in our communion to holding together a variety of judgements on deeply emotive issues. The pacifist must accept as a fellow church member one who differs firmly. If on other ethical judgements we are accustomed to accepting the freedom of individual judgement, it seems difficult to argue that all should agree on this one. Or at least it is difficult to discern the criteria by which one issue might be a cause for church discipline and possible exclusion from church membership and another a matter of tolerance or indifference. There will be private judgement. A question to be asked is: what degree of individual judgement are we prepared to allow in our communities? In some cases individuals will be faced with either sublimating their own views in respect for a commonly owned position held by a congregation, or engaging in active dissent against it. Even more challengingly, in terms of our stated framework, are we as stringent for instance in confronting the first position as we are the fourth?

(2) *The autonomy of the local church*

As far as I am aware it is the declared policy of most Baptist conventions or unions to recognize the autonomy of its member churches, the freedom to govern themselves without interference. The autonomy of the local church is parallel on the corporate level to the freedom of the individual conscience in that it affirms the ability of a community to be led by God without the intervention of an intermediary. As individuals may judge differently so might churches. They are then faced with the same issues as above – to respect a moral judgement made by the wider group to which they belong and sublimate their own mind to it out of respect, or to engage in active dissent. Congregations must be free to do this. Both within and between congregations there are of course boundaries, the crossing of which would be considered so serious to the faith and witness of those congregations that it might lead to withdrawal of co-operation and recognition from a dissenting congregation. On the doctrinal level normative understandings of what it means to be Christian and Baptist function as these boundaries. What degree of difference would there need to be to breach these boundaries in relation to same-sex relations? Within itself the local church is free to determine these boundaries and the hope is that they would be determined by means of a process of theological and ethical reflection rather than by reactive prejudice. The same holds true at the denominational level. Individual conscience and congregational autonomy, however valued, are not absolutes that can function without regard to collective conscience, since all are capable of deviation.

(3) *Determining regional and national policy*

By analogy with the local discerning community, there can be a national policy that is arrived at through the due processes of deliberation and discernment of the relevant communion of churches. Baptists gathered in associations, assemblies or councils have power to discern and decide for precisely the same reason that the local church has: because Christ is in the midst through the Spirit. To be sure, this then has to be willingly received by local congregations and cannot be imposed. In this way the freedom of the local church is safeguarded. However, when what these decisions have to do with relate to intercongregational matters, such as the recognition and accreditation of ministers on a regional or national level, this is clearly within the jurisdiction of the Union, convention or the associations rather than any given local church. It is possible therefore that the communion of churches might lay down a policy in the area of same-sex relations (as is true for instance in the Baptist Union of Great Britain) to which accredited ministers are required to conform and over which they are likely to be disciplined should they breach it. Ministers who disagree with this policy are therefore faced with the choice of sublimating their own views or standing out against it in dissent. Whether or not they will do this no doubt depends on how strongly they feel about the issue and what latitude the policy allows.

(4) Separation of church and state

Baptists have been the strongest advocates of religious freedom and of the separation of the government of the church from the control of the state. This has never meant that they are not deeply committed to the welfare and righteousness of the state. Christians must be free to pursue their vision of a moral and just society and to shape legislation and government accordingly. However, further work needs to be done on the difference between sin and crime. The state must legislate for the actual world, not for an ideal one. Human 'hardness of heart' shapes the nature of legislation and it should neither be considered that what is legal is necessarily right nor that what is wrong should necessarily be made illegal. Where the boundaries are to be drawn is a matter of judgement, but there is no straight line that can be drawn from Christian morality to state legislation. There are not many states in which adultery is punishable in law. The impact of Christian morality upon national laws will be by means of many wavy lines rather than many straight ones. It is certainly the case that the standards the Christian community accepts for itself ought to be considerably higher than those it expects of the state. By its very nature the legislative system will be 'sub-Christian' in the sense that it permits what we personally reject. The law cannot make people good, even if occasionally it is able to put a stop to their wrongdoing. We need to affirm more clearly than we have been in the recent habit of doing that discipleship of Jesus Christ and the proclamation of his redeeming Gospel is the primary focus of the church and that the church's integrity and witness is dependent on its authenticity as a Christian community. Prior then to the question of what kind of state we want is the question of what kind of church do we want. All this is a somewhat oblique way of saying that although Christians may quite legitimately debate the way the state deals with homosexual practice, it is highly questionable if this comes out of a punitive spirit (position one) and must recognize from the start the limited and provisional nature of legislation.

Conclusions

Is there then a distinctively Baptist perspective on homo-sexuality? In terms of substance almost certainly not – we share a range of responses with other traditions. But in terms of process, how we deal with debate and decision, probably so, not uniquely but characteristically so. Let me now summarize what these might be:

- There will be a presumption that conscientious people may judge differently on this contentious issue as they do on others and that they have the right to do so.
- There will be a presumption that local congregations will

seek to discern the mind of Christ and may come to different positions within their own jurisdiction. This too is to be respected.

- There will be recognition that although conscience is free it is not anarchic and that the wider church may test the judgements of individuals and congregations, but not in a punitive or oppressive spirit.
- Where there is difference there will be the attempt to come to agreement about what boundaries to the debate can be agreed upon. Across the span of positions one to four previously discussed, for instance, there will be agreement that casual and promiscuous sex without commitment or compassion are to be rejected.
- Within this there will be a debate about what the mind of the majority is and whether this can be a declared position of the communion of churches as a whole.
- Churches and individuals dissenting from this, or from the mind of local churches, will face hard questions as to whether to sublimate their own views to the discipline of the wider mind in a spirit of submission or whether to dissent from it in the spirit of prophecy.
- As conscience is both individual and corporate it will not always be possible, as it is not on other issues, to avoid hard decisions about the relationship between agreement and co-operation. How much agreement does there have to be to support what quality of co-operation?

I have indicated my own preference in principle for position two with some oscillation in pastoral practice towards position three. It does seem to me that this offers a realistic, principled but sympathetic way forward in a tense and difficult debate. It also seems to strike the right notes in offering moral guidance rooted in moral theology while not losing sight of the persons whose struggle with this issue is all too real. I suggest it could be a meeting ground upon which Baptist Christians with their particular set of instincts and with their differing points of view might find a way of thinking and working together. But the debate needs to be seen also to be about our own identity as a movement. If position four were to be validated, for instance, we would, in my judgement, be defining ourselves as a denomination that sits loose to biblical authority and the consequences of this would be disastrous. However, if we do not maintain the openness to the 'other' and to the struggles people have to maintain their own sexual integrity (expressed in different ways by positions two and three) we would be defining ourselves as a reactionary movement out of touch with real life. A formula to help us in this process might be as follows:

- Concerning position one – we reject it.
- Concerning position four – we decline it.
- Concerning position two – we affirm it.
- Concerning position three – we note it.

The final word has to do with ethics and ecclesiology. All the signs are that as ethical judgements become more and more complex, so the church of tomorrow will have to learn the skills of careful ethical consideration and debate. This requires maturity, wisdom and skill. If the subject matter of this chapter is any indication, the challenge to be genuinely discerning and interpreting communities is one of the greatest we face.

10

Songs of Everlasting Praise

This book has been about identity – who Baptist Christians hope to be at the beginning of the twenty-first century. The subject has been discussed in a variety of ways – theologically, ethically, congregationally. History has been important in describing this identity and so has the future. But the most obvious aspect of our identity has been saved until this final chapter. We, along with all God's people, exist for God's glory and praise.

In the first chapter the claim was made that the true church is yet to come. The true church is that congregation of the redeemed who will be the very dwelling place of the Triune God in the fullness of time. It is something towards which we are moving. The visions of the Book of Revelation (surely a book with a future perspective on things) have the redeemed people of God shouting out the praises of God in a loud voice and in the richest of language.[1] The whole church exists for the glorification of God: Father, Son and Holy Spirit. The song of praise has, of course, already begun. In the worship of the present-day congregation the worship of the new heaven and earth is already anticipated and experienced.

Past, Present, Future

In the Lord's Supper we are most clearly faced with the perspective of time. It is celebrated within the tension of a

---

[1] Revelation 4 – 7.

great memory and a great hope. As bread and wine are shared they enable us to recall those events foundational to the Christian experience that are the means of our salvation – the incarnation and the self-giving in death of Jesus the Christ. These are past events, actions that have happened in history, and have made a difference to the life of humankind ever after. We know of them because of the resurrection of the one who was crucified. Through bread and wine received in the openness of faith we recollect these events that have happened for us and we recall them through the Spirit as the means of our present communion in the life of the Triune God.

But the meal that is shared points forward as well as back. At the Last Supper Jesus gave the promise, 'I will never again drink of this fruit of the vine until that day when I drink it new with you in my Father's kingdom.'[2] In so doing he gave to the celebration of communion an anticipatory character. It is to be seen as a foretaste of the final celebrations that will take place at the restoration of all things, when 'many will come from east and west and will eat with Abraham and Isaac and Jacob in the kingdom of heaven'.[3] It is appropriately therefore not just a time of solemn recollection but of joyful anticipation of the 'marriage supper of the Lamb'.[4] And in being both a recollection and an anticipation it also becomes a moment and a place of present communion with the Christ who having come, and having promised to come again, also comes now to those who are his own and makes himself present to them.[5]

In this exposition of the celebration of communion we also have a pattern for understanding what happens when Christians gather to give their praises to God. They do so in the light of the great acts of salvation, which have been worked for them by the grace of God. In worship the acts are declared and elicit a response. They also gather with an eye to the future –

---

[2] Matthew 26:29.
[3] Matthew 8:11.
[4] Revelation 19:9.
[5] 1 Corinthians 10:16–17.

the glory that is yet to be revealed – and in their praises that future is being tasted and prefigured. And they gather for a living experience in the presence of the Christ who is with those who are gathered in his name and who by means of his mediating work and the Spirit he sends have participation in the divine communion.

The worship of the people of God can therefore be seen to be of incalculable importance. In that worship happens first and foremost for God and God's glory alone, it is 'meet, right and our bounden duty' to give God praise. But it is also the means by which our identity as the children of God is affirmed and sustained; important for our ability to endure as servants of God since in worship the godless influences and pressures of dominant culture are counteracted; significant for sanctification in that in worship we offer ourselves up to the service of God; strategic for mission and outreach since in worship space is opened up in which the Word of God can be spoken and can be heard. Of all the things we do, worshipping God aright is, on anybody's reckoning, high on the agenda.

Identity and Liturgy

This high and strategic perspective on worship has consequences. It leads us to ask how good worship is in Baptist churches. The question begs a variety of supplementary questions. What do we mean by 'good'? Who is to set the standard? If it 'works for me' what right has anybody to question this? These are all very valid. The danger is that we lose ourselves in a mass of subjective preferences and end up saying that anything goes as long as someone likes it somewhere. The way we have outlined communion in past, present and future perspectives ought to give us a place to begin. Worship that is not rooted in the events of Cross and resurrection, that has no future hope and reference, and that does not lead to a living experience of the Christ who is present among his people can surely be declared to be defective –

whatever emotions people may have had evoked for them in a worship service or whatever prescribed liturgical menu they may have followed.

Historically Baptists have had certain instincts in worship. Standing in the Reformed tradition it has been important to them that the reading and explanation of Scripture has a central place – hence the centrality of the pulpit in the older chapels that can still be visited and the astonishing capacity for listening to sermons possessed by the early Baptists. It has been deemed essential that worship should come from the heart. This reflects the voluntarist tradition that has insisted that merely formal or rote religion is not real. People must *feel* what they believe and they must *feel* the worship that they offer. It is not enough to read prayers that somebody else has prepared out of a prayer book since they should reflect not a borrowed experience but a lived one. Immediacy and spontaneity in prayer have been important, not formality. And fellowship has been a highly valued experience. In looking back upon the struggles and privations endured by the earliest Baptists it is difficult at times to see what motivated them to continue. The answer to this is surely that they had discovered in their churches a quality of relating to each other that was of immense importance to them. To call this 'sweet fellowship' sounds to our ears like cloying sentimentality. But in an age when the taste of sweetness was much rarer than it is for us today, and when in a limited diet sweet things would be nourishing rather than fattening, we might see its usefulness in capturing the experience that would have first drawn them and then held them together. The priority of the Word of God, heartfelt devotion and depth of fellowship might still serve as criteria for assessing what amounts from the human perspective to 'good worship'. Churches that are achieving this are not far from where they should be.

Until relatively recently Baptists have regarded themselves as strictly non-liturgical in their approach to worship. But properly no church body, except perhaps the Quakers, is without some kind of liturgy, some way of doing things that is accepted as the norm and provides a way through an act of worship. It will be important to reflect upon the structure of gatherings for worship. However, the overriding concern in this chapter is to argue that what many churches have come to accept as standard approaches to worship are in need of careful rethinking.

The State of Play

There is a widespread concern about the poverty of much that passes for worship among Baptists. 'Formless superficiality' is one way that this poverty has been described to me. The description causes me concern since along the way I have done my bit to bring about changes in worship styles. Nor do I particularly regret those changes, although I am more than willing to recognize that an audit of where we are is appropriate.[6] First of all some kind of historical perspective helps to set the scene.

Earliest Baptist worship was both quite different from what we now find and also different from what many of us might regard as 'traditional' worship in Baptist churches. The first congregations in our tradition were generally quite small, they thrived on being in reaction to the established church, they confined their singing habits to the Psalms (the introduction of hymns in the eighteenth century was a cause of some division), they happily tolerated long sermons (sometimes several in one service), they celebrated communion with alcoholic wine and one cup, they would meet for morning and afternoon services with a meal in between (possibly in the local hostelry), and they would transact their 'business' in close proximity to their worship. Towards the end of the eighteenth and then during the nineteenth centuries styles were slowly updated, hymns

---

[6] Chris Ellis, principal of Bristol Baptist College, has undertaken such an audit and has published it as *Baptist Worship Today* (Didcot, Oxford: Baptist Union of Great Britain, 1999).

were introduced, bands of musicians became common and were then replaced by the organ as buildings became larger and congregations more prosperous. By the beginning of the twentieth century the Baptist liturgical style had become relatively fixed. To refer to it as the 'hymn–prayer sandwich' is both pejorative and accurate. This style is still common in many churches, sometimes in unreconstructed form and at other times with alterations to, for instance, the kind of music used.

This style endured for a considerable time and despite increasingly rapid social change. In the 1960s and 70s it began to change, first of all under the influence of the liturgical movement and then through the charismatic movement. The former brought to a relatively small number a greater sense of liturgical form and decorum. The latter was much more extensive. The introduction of new songs, first to supplement and then to all but replace the older diet of hymns, was accompanied by a shift of mood towards informality and spontaneity. Emphasis upon the gifts of the whole body broadened participation in worship services in both prepared and unprepared ways. Worship became more celebratory, more interactive and joyful, more multimedia, with some use of dance and drama. It also became unpredictably longer. Further quantum leaps were taken in some churches as the overhead projector was introduced and then replaced by the use of PowerPoint. As awareness of spiritual traditions has increased so in the renewal movements that have emerged there has been a broadening of appreciation. Taizé chants and songs from Iona or the world church have broadened and enriched people's repertoire and tolerance in worship and have also led to a convergence of those who might consider themselves in the 'renewal' tradition with those who see themselves as 'liturgical'.

Telling the story of worship in this way makes it sound like unqualified progress. Where then does the charge of 'formless superficiality' come from? This is one of those moments when 'legends of the fall' thinking can distort perception. People forget what we have come out of. What we had was largely a straitjacket that permitted little movement or alteration and proved very resistant to change. Its time was up and it needed to be changed. The tendency now is to compare the best of the old with the worst of the new. This happens not least with many of the hymns and songs that are sung. Some songs are at best of minimal value and are unlikely to endure. When contrasted with the hymns of Wesley and Watts they come off very poorly. But we forget that only a small proportion of the hymns of even the greatest hymn writers are still considered worth singing. They too were capable of doggerel! Conversely, some of the newer material is very good indeed. To imagine that the older forms of worship were stately and rich is to fall prey to false memory syndrome. It was not so.

It is a strength of the shifts in worship style that they do at least reflect the culture and preferences of the present generation. I am personally committed to *popular* worship in the sense that it ought generally speaking to arise out of the cultural expression of ordinary people, not the highbrow choices of a previous generation or of the present-day cultural élite. This is not an argument against tradition but a statement that tradition needs to be reappropriated in the present in an authentic and creative way. Neither is it an argument against the aesthetically high quality of, for instance, a cathedral choir – simply the recognition that this is not where most people are or how they will choose to worship. People may be able to appreciate a wide variety of styles and of music and within the whole worship of the culturally rich people of God there is room for everything. A duty is laid upon us to be exceptionally tolerant in this area. But inevitably people will have ways they find more accessible in which to express themselves liturgically and musically. If worship is to be from the heart it must be through a vehicle that can do justice to what is in the heart. On the other hand, this does not rule out aesthetic considerations. Sloppiness should not be justified on the basis that 'it works for me'. To give God and each other the best that we are capable of is a spiritual imperative. The challenge is to combine these two in authentic, popular and heartfelt worship that is as good as we can make it. There is no excuse for formless superficiality.

Looking to the Future

'Worship wars', in which we stand in judgement upon people's ways of worshipping, are not appropriate. If our perspective is a future one in which we all fall short of the true worship of the true church yet to come then we must all attend to ourselves and our own shortcomings. To decline to be judgemental however should not mean leaving off being discerning. It is an imperative to 'test everything; hold fast to what is good'.[7] Form, language and depth are all significant issues:

As a participant in the charismatic renewal I was once deeply struck by a comment of Professor Andrew Walker in personal conversation that if you took music out of Pentecostalism and the charismatic movement he was not sure how much would be left. It is a useful exercise to apply to the worship of my own tradition. Under the influence of charismatic renewal, music has become so dominant that for many people worship equates to music and singing. From a different angle I have noticed in attending synagogue worship that for Jewish people worship is predominantly about study, of the Torah. The systematic reading of the Hebrew Scriptures is the essence of worship. In visiting mosques I have been struck that for Muslims worship is primarily about prayer. Anybody visiting a Christian church, of probably any Protestant tradition, would conclude that these Christians come together to sing. I have nothing against singing – indeed I enjoy it enormously and believe that when worshippers sing together something can happen of a very spiritual nature. The vision of the church in the Book of Revelation has the church

---

[7] 1 Thessalonians 5:21.

singing a new song.[8] It is good to sing. However, it is also good to have a grasp as to what constitutes worship independently from singing. Worship leading is far more than being able to put a few songs together in some semblance of sequence.

In the early days of the renewal movement those who experienced renewal were very often people who had taken from their training and their experience of earlier styles of worship a sense of structure, movement and development in the conduct of worship. Another word for all of this is 'liturgy'. The generation of those who have succeeded them is very often one that has been brought up in the renewal and does not share the same sense of underlying structure or purpose. The emphasis is placed therefore upon fervency rather than progression. It would be a radical experiment indeed to lay aside completely for a year, say, the use of any kind of music and to discover how worship might be constituted without it. We would be thrust back upon the recitation and study of Scripture and upon prayer in no uncertain terms. We would rediscover the importance of sacrament and ritual moments. We would also in all probability mobilize the gifts and ministries of all the people more intentionally. Structure and the use of the charismata are not in opposition to each other but in each other's service. As an accompanying result we might also find that services are kept shorter, and this might be to the relief of many! Practically speaking it is unlikely that many churches would be able to think of musicless worship, and the intention would never be to give it up permanently but to lay it aside for the sake of strengthening other aspects of worship. But we would all be richer if music were part of an act of worship that contained shape and direction independent of it.

If form is important so is the language that we use. One of the factors that leads to the increasing use of liturgies among traditionally non-liturgical Christians is the sense that the words that we use to celebrate the mystery of God need to be

---

[8] Revelation 5:9,13.

at least partially adequate for the task, rather than ill-thought out and poorly expressed meanderings. While all may be gifted to contribute to the worship of the people of God this does not mean that all are equally gifted in the task of giving expression to the faith we confess. The challenge is to express the content of faith in the best way we can, and it is not the case that anything said by anybody is good enough. Language is potent and powerful. It can detract or magnify. It can obscure the vision of God by calling too much attention to the speaker. It constructs a world and a way of believing. It is best if the language used is simple, economical, sincere and possesses dignity. Ritual moments such as baptism, communion or the blessing of an infant are at their best if the same carefully crafted form of words is used persistently so that it becomes fixed in the minds of the people. These practices become both normative and formative over time. There are certain things that must be said, such as the use of the Triune name in baptism, to give them theological force and content.

Preaching also belongs to this section. The old saying that things must change in order to remain the same surely applies to preaching. The modern world is not sympathetic to preaching and uniformly gives it a bad press. The assumption is that it is boring and there is resentment that any one person should presume to tell others how to live. Yet the modern world also abounds with examples of the power of rhetoric. The sermons of Martin Luther King are part of our cultural history and never cease, in my experience, to inspire. The challenge in this climate is to preach well. Preaching is one of those areas that requires not abandonment but reimagination and the willingness on the part of preachers to update and improve their skills as communicators. As the communication of the message is the end in view and not the mere perpetuation of a cultural style of preaching there is much work to be done here, not least in the development of storytelling, interactive preaching, understanding of how people learn and the skilled use of media, which is now within the reach both financially and technically of most of us.

However within this process it is important not to lose the sense of being 'under the Word': submissive and obedient to the Word that God speaks to us. Not everything can be reduced to a dialogue in which we are equal partners with God. Call and response ought still to have its clear place within the practice of preaching.

And this leads us to think about depth. Worship, however joyful, needs also to be weighty in that it deals in convincing and thoughtful ways with the content of the Christian message and its application to a complex world. God is not in our back pocket. He cannot be reduced to some kind of technique for us to manipulate in our own self-interests. He is not a therapy given to us to improve our psychic health. Christian worship and preaching need to be practical, concerned with the life we live and the world in which we live it. But it must also be profound, taking us beyond ourselves and enabling us to see a bigger picture within which life's lack of resolutions and its mysteries can be placed. Those who preach and those who lead worship have it as part of their responsibility to ensure that depth and quality are achieved. For this reason these are not ministries that everybody can exercise but only those who have maturity of insight into spiritual realities. If the public face of the church is seen in its worship this public face should be one that demands respect and confidence. As a general guide depth in worship comes more readily when we determine to be thoroughly *trinitarian* in our approach to preaching, praying and singing. Superficiality is an accompaniment of the various unitarianisms that are on offer. If the traditional form of Unitarianism is centred on the Father then more recent versions confine themselves either to the Son or to the Spirit so that worship is all about one or the other. But if the worship of the true church in the new heaven and the new earth is to do with being indwelt by and participating in the life of the Triune God then we do well to strive to identify this as an essential aspect of fully Christian worship. To explore the riches of the doctrine of the Trinity and to bear them in mind in leading worship and preaching will rescue many people from superficial thinking.

The Chief End of the Church

The chief end of the church of Jesus Christ is to glorify God on earth as one day God will be glorified in the new heaven and new earth. Worship is the point in space and time in which this calling comes to clearest focus among the people of God. It is therefore a place of orientation and direction, of renewal and rededication. All of this book has been directed towards the end that God's Baptist people might know to what they have been called and how this calling might perhaps be lived out in the first decade of this millennium. There are many other things that might be said. What has been written is here in order to explore not so much who we have been as who we must now be, in the light of our own past and of God's future purpose. Worship finds its communal expression in acts of worship offered to God and from our hearts. But acts of worship lead to lives of worship and service, to lives lived in a certain way because we firmly believe in certain things. As we need God's Spirit to worship truly so we need the same Spirit to live out our worship.

Lord of the church, we pray for our renewing.